FERNANDES

MATT AND TOM OLDFIELD

ULTIMATE
FOOTBALL HEROES

FERNANDES

FROM THE PLAYGROUND
TO THE PITCH

DINO

First published by Dino Books in 2021,
an imprint of Bonnier Books UK,
4th Floor, Victoria House, Bloomsbury Square, London WC1B 4DA
Owned by Bonnier Books,
Sveavägen 56, Stockholm, Sweden

🖸 @dinobooks
🖸 @footieheroesbks
www.heroesfootball.com
www.bonnierbooks.co.uk

Text © Matt Oldfield 2021
The right of Matt Oldfield to be identified as the author of this work has been
asserted by him in accordance with the Copyright, Designs and Patents Act 1988.

Design by www.envydesign.co.uk

Paperback ISBN: 978 1 78946 472 6
E-book ISBN: 978 1 78946 473 3

British Library cataloguing-in-publication data:
A catalogue record for this book is available from the British Library.

Printed and bound in Great Britain by Clays Ltd, Elcograf S.p.A.

1 3 5 7 9 10 8 6 4 2

For all readers,
young and old(er)

ULTIMATE
FOOTBALL HEROES

Matt Oldfield is an accomplished writer and the editor-in-chief
of football review site Of Pitch & Page. Tom Oldfield is a
freelance sports writer and the author of biographies on
Cristiano Ronaldo, Arsène Wenger and Rafael Nadal.

Cover illustration by Dan Leydon.
To learn more about Dan visit danleydon.com
To purchase his artwork visit etsy.com/shop/footynews
Or just follow him on Twitter @danleydon

TABLE OF CONTENTS

ACKNOWLEDGEMENTS

First of all, I'd like to thank everyone at Bonnier Books UK for supporting me throughout and for running the ever-expanding UFH ship so smoothly. Writing stories for the next generation of football fans is both an honour and a pleasure. Thanks also to my agent, Nick Walters, for helping to keep my dream job going, year after year.

Next up, an extra big cheer for all the teachers, booksellers and librarians who have championed these books, and, of course, for the readers. The success of this series is truly down to you.

Okay, onto friends and family. I wouldn't be writing this series if it wasn't for my brother Tom. I owe him so much and I'm very grateful for his belief in me as an author. I'm also very grateful to the rest of my family, especially Mel, Noah, Nico, and of course Mum and Dad. To my parents, I owe my biggest passions: football and books. They're a real inspiration for everything I do.

Pang, Will, Mills, Doug, Naomi, John, Charlie, Sam, Katy, Ben, Karen, Ana (and anyone else I forgot) – thanks for all the love and laughs, but sorry, no I won't be getting 'a real job' anytime soon!

And finally, I couldn't have done any of this without Iona's encouragement and understanding. Much love to you.

CHAPTER 1

MANCHESTER UNITED'S MAGNIFICO

24 January 2021, Old Trafford, Manchester

Bruno was bored and restless. How could he not be when his club, Manchester United, were playing against Liverpool in the FA Cup, and yet he was stuck on the bench? Even though there was no crowd at Old Trafford due to COVID-19, it was still a massive match between English football's biggest rivals, and Bruno desperately wanted to be on the pitch and on the ball, doing what he did best – creating match-winning magic for his team.

'This is stupid,' he muttered to his fellow midfielder Fred, who was a substitute too. 'We should be out there playing!'

Bruno understood that his manager, Ole Gunnar Solskjær, was just trying to give him a rest because of the team's busy schedule, but why couldn't he do that once the season was over? Bruno was one of United's star players with fifteen goals and ten assists, and with a major trophy up for grabs, his team needed him NOW.

'See!' Bruno thought to himself as Mohamed Salah gave Liverpool the lead, but Mason Greenwood soon equalised to make it 1–1. Bruno spent the half-time break warming up, but Solskjær decided to stick with the same team, and three minutes into the second half, Marcus Rashford scored to make it 2–1 to Manchester United.

'Maybe they won't need me today, after all,' Bruno began to wonder, until Salah scored again. *2–2!*

At last, it was time for some changes. First, Liverpool brought on Sadio Mané, and then shortly afterwards, United brought on their star substitute too – Bruno! Right, he had thirty minutes to save the day with some match-winning magic…

'Yes!' he called for the ball straight away. With their Portuguese playmaker on the pitch, United always looked like a much better team: faster, stronger, hungrier, and more likely to score. After one simple sideways pass to Paul Pogba, Bruno moved on to the more adventurous stuff.

PING! He aimed a ball over the top to Marcus, but it didn't quite reach him.

CURL! He delivered a cross towards Edinson Cavani, but a defender headed it away.

Oh well, Bruno was a big believer in the saying, 'If at first you don't succeed, try, try again.' He didn't mind making a few mistakes because eventually he always came up with something special…

With fifteen minutes to go, Edinson won a free kick for United, right on the edge of the Liverpool penalty area. Interesting! Fred and Marcus gathered around the ball too, but there was no doubt who would take it.

'I've got this,' Bruno told them, and they didn't doubt him for a second.

He was feeling even more confident than usual

because the previous day, he had practised his free
kicks for ages after training. Usually, when Bruno
was starting, his manager didn't let him stay out and
do extra work, but seeing as he was a sub for once,
Solskjær had said yes. And so, armed with a big bag of
balls, Bruno had fired off free kick after free kick, just
like he used to during his days as a Sporting Lisbon
superstar. From every angle – left, right, in the middle;
and from every distance – long-range, mid-range, and
close-range, just like this one against Liverpool.

Bruno was feeling positive and well-prepared for
his big moment, but what type of strike would he go
for? Often, he aimed to curl the ball into the top-left
corner, but on this occasion, Edinson gave him some
good advice: 'Try one on the other side – Alisson
won't be expecting it.'

So, when the referee blew his whistle, Bruno fired
the free kick low and hard towards the far corner.
Luckily, his teammates Harry Maguire and Paul Pogba
both ducked at the crucial moment, and so the ball
sailed over them, before dipping down past Alisson's
outstretched arm. *3–2!*

*Goooooooooooooooooooaaaaaaaaaaaaaaaaalllllllllllll
lllllllllll!!!!!!!!!!!!!!!!!!!!!*

A super strike from the super sub! As soon as he
saw the ball hit the back of the net, Bruno raced away
and slid joyfully across the grass.

'Come on, let's go!' he roared as his teammates
threw their arms around him.

'Nice one mate, maybe we should leave you on the
bench more often!' Marcus joked.

Even in an empty stadium, it was still a fantastic
feeling to score a winning goal, and especially a
worldie against a top team like Liverpool. As Bruno
made his way back to the halfway line, he imagined
thousands of ecstatic supporters singing his song:

*Bruno Bruno Bruno,
he's from Sporting like Cristiano.
He goes left, he goes right,
gives defences such a fright,
he's our Portuguese Magnifico!*

He couldn't wait to have the fans safely back at

Old Trafford, but until then, Bruno would do his best to keep entertaining them at home instead. He was determined to become a club legend, like his hero Cristiano Ronaldo, and he was doing a brilliant job so far. Thanks to another moment of magic from their new Portuguese Magnifico, United were heading through to the FA Cup Fifth Round, one step closer to winning a top trophy again.

From Maia to Manchester – what an amazing journey it had been so far for Bruno, and his biggest adventure was only just beginning.

CHAPTER 2

SUNDAY MATCHES IN MAIA

When he reached the end of the street, Ricardo stopped, groaned, and then bounced his football a few times while he waited impatiently for his brother. 'Hurry up, we're nearly there and we haven't got all day!'

'Coming!' Bruno managed to shout back, panting heavily as his trainers slapped against the pavement. He was running as fast as his little six-year-old legs would let him, but he was still trailing behind his big brother, as usual.

At last, they arrived at the local pitch, and Bruno was able to slow down and get his breath back – but not for long.

'Right, everyone ready?' Ricardo called out to the group of kids who were already gathered there. At the age of eleven, he was one of the oldest there, and as he had his own ball, he was the leader too. 'Let's get started because the grown-ups will be here soon!'

The Sunday match was a local tradition in Maia, Portugal, where the Fernandes brothers lived. It was seen as a social event, the chance for people to enjoy themselves after a hard week of work, and forget about all their problems for a while. Although Bruno's family didn't have much money, one thing they did have was a love of football. Later on, their father, José, who worked long hours in a textile factory, would play in the adult game with friends and family, but first, it was the kids' turn to take to the field. In a flash, the two teams were picked, and their match was kicking off.

'Let's play!'

Bruno had been waiting for this moment all week: the chance to show off his new and improving football skills. Thanks to hours of watching and copying his brother, he was getting better and better at the basics

– ball control, passing, tackling, dribbling, shooting. Even his dad said so, but could he impress Ricardo with his progress in the Sunday match, when it really mattered? They were playing on the same team, so the timing was perfect.

First, however, Bruno needed to get the ball. Every time the other team had it, he chased after it, and every time his team had it, he called for it:

'Over here, I'm free!'

'Pass it to me – I'll pass back, I promise!'

But it was no use; the older players like Ricardo kept hogging it, refusing to pass to a little six-year-old like him. Bruno didn't give up, though; oh no, he was going to become the best footballer in Maia, better than his brother, better than his dad, even better than his brilliant cousin Vítor. That was his dream, and he was determined to achieve it.

First, however, he still needed to get the ball…

'NEXT GOAL WINS!' Ricardo shouted, the signal that their time on the pitch was almost over. All the grown-ups were now there on the sidelines, watching and waiting to play.

For Bruno, it was now or next weekend, which felt like forever away to him. So, with the last of his energy, he sprinted towards his opponent who had the ball once more, stretched out his leg, and this time, he successfully made the tackle!

Nice one, Bruno!

Woah, what next? As he dribbled forward, he could hear the opposition defenders chasing after him, but he tried not to panic. This was his golden opportunity to be the matchwinner, and he wasn't going to waste it.

Go on, Bruno!

But by the time he entered the penalty area, it felt like he'd run a marathon already, and he still had the goalkeeper left to beat. Was he really good enough to go for glory himself? What if he messed it up and missed the match-winning shot? Where were his teammates when he needed them…?

'Bruno, I'm here!'

It was Ricardo, who had raced all the way forward from defence to help him. Phew! Bruno played the pass just in time before the keeper dived at his feet, leaving his brother with an open...

GOOOOOAAAAAALLLLLL!

They had done it; together, the Fernandes brothers had won the Sunday match in Maia, and they celebrated like it was the World Cup final. For Bruno, it was the new number one greatest moment of his whole life.

'Next week, we'll go on the same team again,' Ricardo told him excitedly, 'and we'll score lots more goals!'

José clapped and cheered proudly as his sons walked off the pitch arm-in-arm. 'Well done, boys, what teamwork – it's good to see that football runs in the family!'

Bruno and Ricardo stayed at the pitch to watch their dad play, but neither of them could really concentrate on the game. Instead, they both stood there on the sidelines replaying their winning goal in their heads, while also dreaming about the day when they would be old enough – and good enough – to play with the grown-ups in the main Saturday match.

For Ricardo, that day was probably only a couple of

years away, but for Bruno it would be a much longer wait. That was okay, though; he still had lots more practising to do first.

CHAPTER 3

DETERMINED TO BE THE BEST

To prepare for the Sunday matches in Maia, the Fernandes brothers played and played for hours every day out in the streets below the family apartment. They were both football mad and determined to be the best young players in the town. If enough of Ricardo's friends were around, they would play five-a-side games in any free space they could find, dodging any people, dogs, or cars passing by. Although Bruno was usually the youngest and the smallest player there, that didn't bother him at all. He just wanted to play football and he wasn't afraid of anything, not even nutmegging the big boys.

'You're going to pay for that, Bruno!'

If everyone else was busy, the brothers just practised one-on-ones instead, which could be even more intense and competitive. Their battles often ended in angry arguments because both were so desperate to win and avoid the worst thing in the world: losing to a brother. That could put them in a bad mood for days.

'Hey, that's a foul!'

'No way, I got the ball!'

'Whatever, I'm going to make you look like a fool next time!'

Ricardo was five years older, so he had the extra strength and experience, but his younger brother was catching him up quickly, especially when it came to skills. Bruno was already a little magician on the ball, and he was getting better and better. In their street games, the others tried and tried to tackle him, but some days they just couldn't get the ball off him. Then with a flash of his feet, Bruno would skip past them with a clever stepover or a cheeky nutmeg. *Olé!*

'If you keep this up, you could be the next Rui Costa or Luís Figo!' his friends predicted, feeling a combination of admiration and frustration.

Bruno too supported the Portugal national team, but after their poor performance at the 2002 World Cup, he had found a new football hero: Ronaldinho. Not only was the Brazil and Barcelona star a phenomenal player but with his outrageous skills and smiling face, he made the game look so easy, exciting, and entertaining. Bruno could happily watch him for hours! And he would, carefully studying every single unbelievable trick and flick, so that he could go out and copy it in the streets.

'Woah, when did you learn to do that?' Ricardo asked as his brother flicked the ball one way and then the other to fool him with two super-fast touches. It really did look like magic.

'Yesterday,' Bruno replied proudly; all his hard work had been worth it. 'It's called an Elástico – it's one of Ronaldinho's favourites!'

Day by day, he was building up his box of tricks by learning from his heroes: first Ricardo and their cousin Vítor, then Ronaldinho, and soon there was a third, and this time one from Bruno's own country.

Cristiano Ronaldo was a promising young winger just starting out at Sporting Lisbon when in 2003 he signed for one of the biggest clubs in the world – the eight-time English Premier League Champions, Manchester United.

'Imagine how amazing that must be?!' Bruno marvelled with his brother. Playing for Manchester United, alongside the likes of Rio Ferdinand, Paul Scholes, Ryan Giggs and Ruud van Nistelrooy, was every young football fan's dream.

Bruno had only watched Cristiano play a few times on TV, but he already loved his style: fast, fearless and a real flair player, who could weave his way past any poor defender who had to face him. Even at a young age, Cristiano was confident enough to show off his full range of skills – just like Bruno himself! He couldn't wait to see what Ronaldo did next.

'I support Manchester United now!' Bruno told all his friends.

It wasn't easy to watch English football in Portugal at that time, especially for the Fernandes family because money was always tight. But Bruno did whatever he could to follow Cristiano's progress, as he went from a skilful show-off to a goal-scoring machine and a Champions League winner. Wow, what a success story! It was the perfect inspiration for Bruno as he set out on his own club football career.

CHAPTER 4

IMPROVING AT INFESTA

From the very first training session, the Futebol Clube Infesta youth coach Sergio Marques could see that Bruno was a very talented footballer. The skinny eight-year-old had all the skills, and he wasn't scared to show them off. Even on day one, he dominated the practice match, telling his new teammates what to do and demanding the ball from them.

'No, not to him – pass it to *ME!*'

'What was that? I was free!'

While Marques was impressed by Bruno's confidence, he could see there was work to do in order to turn him into a better team player. Dribbling and shooting were important skills, but he had to be good at passing, heading, and tackling too. Football is a team game, and so the Infesta coach set about showing Bruno that he couldn't do everything on his own.

There were two main parts to Marques's plan. The first involved Bruno's position on the pitch. Like a lot of young footballers, he wanted to be an attacking midfielder, and in some matches, his manager let him play there. But in their most difficult games, Marques didn't want Bruno hogging the ball and always trying to be the hero, so he moved his star player into central defence.

'Me, a defender?!' Bruno argued at first, but in fact, it turned out to be a very clever tactic. From the back, he could lead the team better, organising everyone around him and starting the attacks. Plus, in defence, he could really show off his determination and desire to win, even if his competitive spirit did get him into trouble sometimes.

'Bruno, if you don't calm down, you're going to get sent off,' his coach often had to warn him.

'Fine, but that was never a foul – the ref got it wrong!'

With Bruno excelling at centre-back, Marques moved on to the second part of his plan, which involved lots more practice. The best young players were always looking to learn, but what about Bruno? At Infesta, he was already training three nights a week, plus playing matches every Saturday, but when his coach asked if he wanted to do some extra one-to-one sessions to work on his weaknesses, he agreed straight away. The chance to play more football?

'Yes please! How soon can we start?'

While Bruno loved nothing more than dribbling with the ball all game long, he was also eager to improve as an all-round player. He knew that he still had a long way to go if he wanted to be 'The Next Ronaldo' one day. So, together with his coach, Bruno spent his Tuesday nights working hard on his:

Passing:

'That's it, look up and find the gaps.'

Ball control:

'Get your first touch right, and everything else will follow.'

Heading:

'If you time your jump well, it doesn't matter how tall your opponent is.'

And Tackling:

'You don't always have to dive in. Sometimes, it's best to stay on your feet and wait.'

All that extra advice and practice paid off because week after week, Bruno got better and better. He still liked to be Infesta's main man on the pitch whenever possible, but winning was the most important thing, and if sometimes that meant stepping back and creating chances for others, then he didn't mind at all.

'Brilliant, Bruno – what an assist!'

Marques was the first to notice the improvement, then his teammates, and then their opponents. Wow, what a talent! Now that he was an all-action, all-round star, Bruno was unstoppable. Before long, he was stealing the show at the top local tournaments, playing so well that scouts from Boavista and Porto, two of Portugal's biggest rivals, spoke to his parents about signing him.

'Really?' Bruno's eyes were already wide with excitement, but he had to double-check that his dad was telling the truth.

Jorge nodded back with pride and joy. 'Yes, son – they believe you're a superstar in the making. As I always say, football runs in the family!'

Boavista or Porto – which one would Bruno choose? It was going to be a hard decision, but either way, he was heading in the right direction, moving one step closer to achieving his dream of becoming a professional football player.

CHAPTER 5

BIG MOVE TO...
BOAVISTA!

Boavista or Porto? Boavista or Porto? It was a really big decision that could affect his whole career, so Bruno was determined to get it right.

Although Boavista had won Portugal's Primeira Liga back in 2001, Porto were a much more successful football team. They had won the League twenty times, including the last two seasons in a row! Plus, under their current manager, José Mourinho, the club had also recently won the UEFA Cup and the Champions League. Vítor Baía, Fernando Couto, Hélder Postiga, Ricardo Carvalho, Deco – it was the home of so many of Portugal's best players, past and present.

'What's there to think about?' most of his friends

told him. 'Of course, you should sign for Porto!'

But Bruno wasn't so sure because he had a real soft spot for Boavista. Their ground, the Estádio do Bessa, was only six miles away from Maia, and he had been there many times as a supporter. He loved being part of the atmosphere there, cheering the team on to victory. Boavista really felt like home to him, especially as his cousin and football hero, Vítor Borges, had been playing there for years. Bruno had been there watching at the Estádio do Bessa when Vítor made his first-team debut.

'Come join me,' Vítor urged Bruno. 'You'll love it here – we can become Boavista heroes together!'

It had always been Bruno's dream to follow in Vítor's footsteps, and this was his opportunity. Plus, wouldn't he have a better chance of breaking into the first team and becoming a professional footballer at Boavista than at a bigger club like Porto?

For days, Bruno kept thinking and then re-thinking, until eventually, a deal was done. In the end, his decision came down to transport, as well as football. The Fernandes family didn't own a car, and Boavista had offered to pick Bruno up and take him to and from every training session and match. Not only would that save him lots of long, boring bus rides, but it also showed that the club really cared about him.

'Okay – I've made up my mind,' Bruno told his parents.

At the age of ten, he was signing for Boavista! He was going to become a star for his local football team and the fans would sing songs about him at the Estádio do Bessa. That was his big plan but first, he went back to say an emotional goodbye to everyone at Infesta, his first football club, including his first football coach who had really helped him to improve.

'Thanks for everything,' he told Marques as they hugged. 'I'm really going to miss playing here!'

'We're going to miss you too,' Marques replied. 'Good luck, kid – go and become an even greater player at Boavista!'

'Don't worry, Coach – I will!'

As Bruno arrived at his new club, he was brimming with confidence and enthusiasm. Yes, the Boavista youth team would be a big step-up from Infesta, but he was ready to work hard and was determined to succeed. He would listen as carefully to his new coaches as he had to Marques, and show that he was a talented player and a fast learner. Whatever they asked him to do, he would do with total dedication – even being a ball boy at the Estádio do Bessa!

Play as a striker? Sure, why not? Bruno had always had a really powerful and accurate shot, which he used in order to score lots of goals for the Boavista youth teams.

Play as a midfielder? Yes please! Midfield playmaker was still Bruno's favourite position because he got to be on the ball all the time, doing a bit of everything: passing, tackling, dribbling and shooting. In the Number 8 role, he was always involved in the game, and he could really show off those all-round skills that he'd worked on with Marques. Boavista had lots of brilliant young midfielders, though, so often they asked him to...

Play as a defender? No problem! After all, it was a role that Bruno knew well from his days at Infesta. And if the coaches thought that was the position where he had the best chance of becoming a professional, then he was happy to make it his own. He would lead from the back and battle fiercely for every ball, before dribbling his way out of defence or playing perfect long passes.

Play as a keeper? No, fortunately the Boavista coaches never asked Bruno to go in goal, but he would have happily worn the gloves and given it 110 per cent effort if they had.

'Maybe you should give it a try – you're always diving around, anyway!' his teammates teased him in training.

Bruno smiled but he didn't say no. He was determined to play professional football one day, no matter what his position on the pitch.

CHAPTER 6

FOCUSED ON HIS FOOTBALL DREAM

With the ball tucked under his arm, Bruno darted along the school corridor as fast as he could. Why couldn't they just make break-times much longer? Twenty minutes was never enough for a proper football match, and once Bruno and his friends started playing, it was so hard to stop. Time flies when you're having fun, and now he was in trouble. His next lesson had already begun, but if he was lucky, he might be able to sneak into the classroom without the teacher noticing…

'Ah, there you are,' Ms Almeida said with a sigh, standing watch at the door. 'You're late… AGAIN!'

'Sorry, Miss,' he panted, while wiping the sweat off

his forehead. 'We were playing a game and I—'

'No, I don't want to hear your football stories, Bruno. As you can see, class has started – quickly go and put your ball away and wash your face, so that you're ready to learn.'

'Yes, Miss.'

Bruno was on his best behaviour for the rest of the lesson, but he couldn't concentrate on what Ms Almeida was saying. As usual, there was something else on his mind: football! He thought back over the match he had just played at school – the mistakes he had made, as well as his most magical moments – and then forward to his next game for Boavista. What could he do better? How could he impress his coaches? The squad was so competitive that he needed to keep improving every week.

At last, the bell rang, but as he sprinted towards the door...

'Bruno, can you stay behind for a minute please?'

Noooo! Lunchtime was only an hour long and his precious football time was already ticking away...

Ms Almeida waited for all the other students to

leave before she spoke: 'Look, I know how much you love football and I know you're doing well at Boavista, but you need to have a Plan B in life, just in case things don't work out. That's why your education is so important. I'm not saying you have to stop playing football – no way! What I'm saying is you need to try to find a better balance between your football and your schoolwork.'

Bruno nodded glumly. Ms Almeida was right; there was no reason why he couldn't do well at both.

'I'll work harder, Miss, I promise.'

'Good. Now, off you go and play!'

While Bruno did increase his efforts at school, he stayed focused on his football dream. He believed in himself, even if others didn't, and besides, becoming a professional player was the only thing he wanted to do with his life. It was the path to fame and glory, but also a better future for him and his struggling family.

Times were hard in Portugal, and as a result, lots of people had lost their jobs, including Bruno's dad. What was the Fernandes family going to do now? Without his wages from the factory, how would they have enough money for food? José looked and looked for another job – in Maia, in Porto, in the capital city, Lisbon – but it was no use. It seemed like the only option was to move away and start again in another country.

'Switzerland?' Bruno couldn't believe what he was hearing. At the age of fourteen, his parents were asking him to wave goodbye to his friends and to his football dream. What were they expecting him to say – 'Yes, no problem'? Well, they were wrong. Instead, he stormed out of the room, shouting, 'No way, I'm not going – they don't even know how to play football there!'

Bruno couldn't name a single Swiss club, or even a single player, whereas he knew everything about the Primeira Liga and its superstars. Portugal was his home, and his future was there. He couldn't give up now, not when he had worked so hard, and was on his way to becoming the next Cristiano Ronaldo. In a few years' time, he could be playing for the Boavista first team!

Bruno's parents José and Virginia tried to persuade

him that moving away was for the best, but when it came to football, he wouldn't budge. He even threatened to run away from home, until in the end, he got his way. While José set off for a new job in Switzerland, the rest of the family stayed behind in Maia.

'Good luck, kid!' José told Bruno as they said their goodbyes. He could completely understand his son's decision; he was sure that he would have done the same thing himself in that difficult position. 'I'm sorry I won't be around for a while, but I'll be supporting you all the way. Make me proud at Boavista!'

It was a sad situation, but it made Bruno even more determined to achieve his football dream. He had to succeed, for the sake of his separated family.

CHAPTER 7

PASTELEIRA'S PLAYMAKER

At first, Bruno didn't mind playing in defence for the Boavista youth teams, but as the years went by, he grew more and more frustrated. Why couldn't he just play in his favourite position? He wanted to move further up the pitch, where he could control the game more.

Bruno knew that he was never going to be a powerful forward like his number one football hero Cristiano Ronaldo, but surely he could be a classy, creative midfielder like Rui Costa or Portugal's next young star, João Moutinho? At that time, Moutinho was playing for Porto, which meant that Bruno could watch him on TV every week. And the more he saw, the more he thought, 'Yes, that's the kind of footballer I want to be!'

At the heart of the midfield, Moutinho was on the ball more than any other player on the pitch, but he hardly ever lost it or wasted it. Every touch was excellent, and almost every pass was perfect, whether short or long, to the left, right or through the middle. His role in the team was really important – to be the link between the defence and attack – but he made it look so simple and fun.

Bruno was mesmerised, as if he were looking at an amazing work of art. On the TV screen, he studied Moutinho's every move – the runs he made, the looks he gave to see who was around him, the way he used his body to protect the ball, and the way he swung his leg as he played another defence-splitting pass.

'I could definitely do all that too!' Bruno thought to himself, daring to dream.

The problem was, though, that the Boavista youth team already had plenty of brilliant players in that position, including a new kid signed from Porto called André Gomes. There didn't seem to be any space for Bruno, so what should he do? If he didn't say something soon, he might get stuck in defence for the rest of his football career. Nooo – he couldn't let that happen. So, eventually, Bruno decided to be brave and speak up:

'Coach, I want to be a midfielder.'

As he'd predicted, there wasn't a place for him at Boavista, but there was at Pasteleira, one of the smaller local clubs they were connected with. Would he want to go there on loan?

'Yes please!' Bruno decided and his timing could not have been better. With the new season about to start, the Pasteleira coach Antonio Peres was going through his squad, looking for gaps he needed to fill. And there was one thing they really needed: a Number 10. Where were they going to find a new attacking playmaker, someone capable of scoring great goals and creating them too?

'I can do that!' Bruno told his new coach with total confidence.

'Really, I thought you said you were a midfielder, a Number 8?' Peres replied warily. He wasn't yet sure about this new kid with the long, flowing hair – was he really as good as he seemed to think he was?

'Yeah, I can play there too, but just give me a chance in the Number 10 role,' Bruno pleaded. Perhaps he could even combine the two roles into one, like another of his new heroes, Barcelona's Andrés Iniesta. 'I promise I won't let you down!'

And he didn't. Bruno became an instant success as Pasteleira's new playmaker, scoring in almost every single game, and setting up lots more goals for the strikers too. Now that he was free to go wherever he wanted on the pitch, he felt like a totally different player – much happier and much more dangerous.

In no time at all, Bruno was back to being the boss of his team, telling everyone else what to do, just like he had in his earlier days at Infesta.

'No, not to him – pass it to *ME!*'

'Why did you shoot from there? Look up next time!'

Yes, he could be annoying at times, but Bruno always led by example, chasing every ball and inspiring the other Pasteleira players to do the same. After a while, his teammates didn't know what they'd done without him.

'You lost a lot more matches, that's what!' Bruno told them with a cheeky grin.

At Pasteleira, he finally felt at home again, somewhere he could show his true self – fun, friendly, and passionate about football, but also competitive, argumentative, and one of the worst losers in the world.

'Hey, that was a foul! Are you trying to injure me?'

'No, that ball crossed the line, and you know it!'

In training, Peres sometimes had to send his star player off to cool down and stop him from fighting with his own teammates. And in matches, the Pasteleira coach sometimes had to calm Bruno down before the referee showed him a red card. Bruno wasn't afraid to argue with Peres either, but his anger never lasted too long after the final whistle.

'Sorry, Coach, I didn't mean what I said. I was just—'

'I know, you were in the heat of the match and you wanted to win. Don't worry about it.'

One thing that Peres did worry about, though, was Boavista asking for Bruno to come back. Surely, it was only a matter of time before they called because the kid was far too talented to keep playing at Pasteleira forever. Peres had no doubt that the boy had the talent and determination to make it as a professional footballer. He was something special.

And Bruno believed that too. By the age of fifteen, he was ready to return to Boavista, with his head held high and a point to prove. It was time to fight for the right to be the club's best young playmaker.

CHAPTER 8

"MARADONA OF NOVARA"

Things were going really well for Bruno, both on and off the football pitch. Boavista had welcomed him back and he was working his way towards the first team, while playing in his favourite position. Plus, when he moved schools to be closer to the club's training ground, he met Ana Pinho, the love of his life.

Bruno fell for her as soon as he saw her in class, and when he plucked up the courage to speak to her, those feelings grew stronger and stronger. It hadn't been easy to impress her – no, 'I play football for Boavista' didn't work – but eventually, Ana had agreed to go on a date with him, and the rest was history. Now, when Bruno wasn't playing football, the pair were inseparable, and soon, they were part of each other's families too.

'Bruno, I know you love Boavista, but have you thought about playing for bigger clubs in other countries?' Ana's brother Miguel said one day as they sat chatting about football.

Of course, he had! Bruno's big dream was to follow in Cristiano Ronaldo's footsteps and play in the Premier League, but he was trying to take things one step at a time. He was still only sixteen, after all.

'Yeah, one day – for now, though, I'm just focusing on getting into the Boavista first team.'

'Come on, you've got to aim higher than that!' Miguel urged. 'That's why a brilliant young player like you needs an agent like me. We're basically brothers now, anyway! So, what do you say?'

Bruno smiled, but he didn't say yes or no.

'Okay, well let me speak to some people I know,' Miguel said mysteriously, 'and then we'll talk again soon.'

One of those people turned out to be Cristiano Giaretta, the Sporting Director at Novara, a football club in the north of Italy. As one of the smaller teams in Serie A, the country's top division, they were always on the lookout for promising young players they could develop into multimillion-Euro superstars. So, Giaretta sent the head of the Novara academy, Mauro Borghetti, to Portugal to watch Bruno in action for the Boavista Under-19s.

'If he's as good as Miguel says, he should be the best player on the pitch!'

After the first ten minutes, Borghetti had picked out the best player, and it wasn't Bruno. Yes, the boy was skilful, but so were lots of other young footballers, and he didn't seem to have anything special about him, like super-speed or strength.

'Oh well, worth a look,' Borghetti muttered to himself, 'but he's not right for Novara.'

As the match went on, however, Bruno got more and more involved in the game, until at last, Borghetti saw what was special about him – his strong character. The boy was a born leader and a real fighter on the pitch, fearless in the tackle and fearless on the ball too. He played the game in such a positive way. So what if a dribble didn't work, a pass got intercepted, or a shot went wide? He was brave enough to keep trying until he eventually succeeded.

'Hmm, maybe I was wrong about him,' Borghetti began to think.

The boy had a big personality and he really showed it on the pitch. He didn't stop battling until the final whistle blew and his team had won. By then, Borghetti had changed his mind completely.

'We should sign him straight away,' he told Giaretta enthusiastically. 'I really think he's a Serie A superstar in the making!'

Novara quickly agreed a fee with Boavista, who were in desperate need of money – €40,000. What a bargain that could be, but would Bruno be willing to make the move?

***

'Novara? Are they an Italian team?'

It wasn't the really positive response that Miguel had been hoping for when he gave Bruno the good news, but he kept going anyway:

'Yes, they were in Serie A last season – they beat Inter Milan, remember? But unfortunately, they got relegated and now they want you to help get them back there! It's an amazing opportunity to play first-team football and make a name for yourself in Italy – think about it.'

Bruno did, and he also discussed it with Ana. He was still only seventeen and moving to another country would be scary, especially without her.

'Don't worry,' Ana reassured him. 'I'll come and visit you as often as I can!'

So, with a mix of nerves and excitement, Bruno bravely set out on his big Italian adventure. His mum travelled with him to complete the transfer and help him settle into his new home. But after a few days, Virginia returned to Portugal, leaving Bruno all alone in a foreign city.

At first, he found things really hard – he didn't know anyone in Novara, and he didn't speak any Italian either. How was he supposed to talk to his teammates, or understand the coach's instructions?

But instead of just giving up and going back to Portugal, Bruno turned to his special power – his strong character. He refused to be defeated, especially when it came to football.

Everyone else spoke Italian? Right, well, he would just have to learn the language too then! Bruno put up post-it notes all over his bedroom at Hotel Novarello, the club's training ground, with important Italian words written on them. One month later, he could speak the language well enough to have a decent conversation.

'Molto bene, Bruno!'

His coaches were impressed by his talent and determination, and so were his teammates. Bruno started out in the Novara Under-19s, but he didn't stay there long. After a hat-trick on his debut and two more goals against Cagliari, he was quickly moved up to train with the first-team squad. Progress!

Once he got there, though, Bruno didn't just walk straight into the Novara starting line-up. No, even though the club were closer to relegation than promotion, he had to wait patiently for his opportunities. After making his debut as a late substitute, another eight league games passed before he got another chance to play. Why? Because his coaches were worried that he was too small and skinny for life in Serie B.

By February 2013, however, Bruno had forced his way into the team and with his creativity and drive at the heart of their midfield, Novara were flying up the table:

from fifteenth place...

Bruno grabbed his first assist in a win over Juve Stabia,

...up to eleventh...

He scored back-to-back goals against Spezia and Ternana,

...to eighth...

Even when he didn't get on the scoresheet, he was still at the centre of everything,

...then sixth...

He only came on in the second half, but he still managed to score one and set another up against Cittadella,

…and finally, fifth!

In only the second minute of their crucial match against league leaders Sassuolo, Bruno raced forward, calling for the ball as usual. When it arrived, he was still thirty yards from goal, but he thought, 'why not?' BANG! With the outside of his right foot, he fired a ferocious shot straight into the top corner. 1–0!

Gooooooooooooooooooooaaaaaaaaaaaaaaaaalllllllllllllll llllllllllll!!!!!!!!!!!!!!!!!!!!!!

What a wonderstrike! As the crowd in the Stadio Silvio Piola went wild, Bruno raced over to the corner flag, with his teammates trailing behind. When he got there, he slid on his knees in front of the Novara fans.

'Come onnnnnnn!' he cried out, pumping his fists with passion. His brave move to Italy had turned out to be a brilliant idea. From a lower mid-table position, he had helped lift his team all the way to the Serie B play-offs, in only three months. No wonder the local newspapers were calling him the 'Maradona of Novara'!

Sadly, the club's incredible run came to an end in the play-offs against Empoli. So close! Novara would be staying in Serie B after all, but not their Portuguese midfield maestro. No, after his breakthrough half-season, Bruno was on his way to Serie A.

CHAPTER 9

SERIE A'S NEXT SUPERSTAR?

Udinese were the Serie A team who won the race to sign Bruno that summer, largely thanks to their new Sporting Director – Giaretta! One of his first tasks when he arrived at Udinese was to go back to Novara and buy their brightest young star, the Portuguese playmaker he had helped bring to Italy in the first place.

'Trust me, he's a special talent!' Giaretta told everyone else at his new club.

Although Novara were sad to see Bruno leave so soon, at least they made a decent profit: €1 million was always welcome at a small club like theirs. 'Good luck!' the coaches and players said as they waved him goodbye.

Bruno was pleased with his progress – one year in Italy, and he was already going up in the world. Udinese were a much bigger team and that meant bigger wages too. The club even gave him a car as a gift when he signed! And on the pitch in Serie A next season, he would be battling for the ball against Roma's Miralem Pjanić, Napoli's Marek Hamšík, and, best of all, Juventus's legendary playmaker Andrea Pirlo, another of Bruno's midfield heroes, who he had loved watching and learning from for years.

Luckily, though, Bruno would have top teammates around him to help. The previous season, Udinese had finished fifth in Serie A and qualified for the Europa League. The squad was packed with quality players, led by club captain and Italian legend, Antonio Di Natale, or 'Toto' as everyone called him. The thirty-six-year-old striker had scored over twenty league goals for the last four years in a row.

Aside from Di Natale, though, Udinese were most famous for discovering future superstars from all over the world, developing their skills, and then selling them on to bigger clubs. In recent years, Chilean

Alexis Sánchez had gone to Barcelona, Columbian
Juan Cuadrado had signed for Fiorentina, Slovenian
Samir Handanović had moved to Inter Milan, Ghanaian
Kwadwo Asamoah had joined Juventus, and Moroccan
Medhi Benatia had moved to Roma. Perhaps their new
Portuguese playmaker would be next?

Bruno was still only eighteen, but he had no
intention of staying in the Udinese Under-19s. No
way, he was determined to play first-team football
as soon as possible, just like he had at Novara. If he
could shine in Serie B, why couldn't he do the same
in Serie A? He was ready and raring to go.

The Udinese manager, Francesco Guidolin, saw
it straight away at the pre-season training camp. For
a youngster who had only just arrived from a lower
league, Bruno played with such positivity and belief.
Instead of shyly waiting for others to pass to him, he
took responsibility and got on the ball as much as
possible.

'This kid could be something special,' Guidolin
thought to himself.

With his pet Labrador Simba to keep him company,

Bruno soon settled into life at a new club in a new city, and before long, Ana joined him too. Much better! By then, he was already sitting on the subs bench for the first-team most weeks, but with Ana, his soon-to-be wife, by his side, he was ready to push on to the next level: a place in the starting line-up.

He worked hard and learned fast in practice, but unfortunately for him, Udinese had a very fixed first XI and formation. How was Guidolin going to fit Bruno into the system? The manager preferred to have two strikers up top – Toto and Luis Muriel – and a midfield three featuring only one creative playmaker, Roberto Pereyra. So, there was no space for young Bruno... for now. But while the system had worked well the previous season, this time around, it wasn't so successful. Udinese were ninth in the table, and they had only scored ten goals in their opening ten games.

When his team went 2–0 down at home to Inter Milan, Guidolin knew that he had to make some changes. So early in the second half, he went for a double substitution:

Off went Toto and on came Mathias Ranégie,

And off went Roberto and on came… Bruno!

At last! Bruno raced out onto the pitch, determined to make an instant impact in the remaining thirty minutes. Although it was too late to save Udinese from defeat, he still impressed his manager with his energy and his confidence on the ball. With time running out, he weaved his way through two Inter midfielders and then struck a long-range shot that Handanović had to dive down and save.

'Unlucky, good effort!' Guidolin clapped and cheered.

Toto would be out injured for the next game against Catania, so the Udinese manager decided to try something different – one striker up top, with two attacking midfielders in behind: Roberto and Bruno. Hurray, he had made it into the starting line-up! They lost the first match, but Guidolin kept faith in his new formation, and in his new Portuguese playmaker too. Because game after game, Bruno was getting better and better.

Away at Napoli, Udinese were 2–0 down and heading for another defeat, until Bruno led the fightback. Even as the new kid, aged just eighteen, he wasn't afraid to show his strong character and take charge. First, his high, curling corner caused an own goal, and then with twenty minutes to go, he picked up the ball and dribbled forward, looking for a clever pass to play. When he couldn't see one, he decided to shoot instead. BANG! From outside the penalty area, his powerful shot swerved up over the goalkeeper's upstretched arm and then dipped down into the net. *2–2!*

Gooooooooooooooooooooaaaaaaaaaaaaaaaalllllllllllllll llllllllllll!!!!!!!!!!!!!!!!!!!!

'Come on!' Bruno screamed, sprinting over to the supporters. What a way to score his first goal for Udinese, and thanks to him, they were right back in the game!

That wondergoal was enough to get everyone in Italy talking. Bruno Fernandes – was he going to be Serie A's next superstar?

Guidolin did his best to protect his young playmaker and give him plenty of rest, but Bruno was just too brilliant to leave out of the team for long. Udinese were winning 1–0 when he came on against Verona. Twenty minutes later, it was 3–0, and Bruno had another goal and an assist.

'You're a real gamechanger!' Roberto shouted as they celebrated together.

But it wasn't just the big, glory moments that made Bruno such an important part of the team. It was also his all-round play – the tireless running, the clever movement, the quick thinking on the ball, and of course, the incredible will to win.

'Honestly, I've never met anyone who hates losing as much as you!' Toto told him with a smile of respect.

Although Udinese finished the Serie A season in thirteenth place, with Bruno running the show in midfield, the club's future looked bright.

CHAPTER 10

STILL LOTS TO LEARN

'Bruno is very young and has more ability than any of us. He's got two incredible feet but sometimes he drifts through games.'

Toto was just letting out his frustration after another Udinese defeat, but his words still hurt because Bruno knew that his teammate was right. After his successful first season in Italy's top division, everyone was expecting him to keep getting better and better – more goals, more assists, more match-winning moments.

Bruno was hoping for lots more Serie A success too, but instead, 2014–15 turned out to be a difficult second season for him. Yes, he had scored an excellent solo strike against Cesena and an incredible volley in a 2–1 win away at Inter Milan, and yes, he had curled in a beautiful cross for Toto against Verona, but Udinese needed a lot more than that from their main playmaker. For all his fancy footwork and flashes of brilliance, Bruno wasn't yet dominating games in midfield, and so under new manager Andrea Stramaccioni, he often found himself sitting on the bench instead.

'I'm going backwards, not forwards!' he grumbled to Ana as his team slipped further and further down the Serie A table.

No-one was calling him 'The New Iniesta' anymore, but Bruno never gave up. He was determined to turn things around, and on the final day of the season, he got the chance to return to the starting line-up. As half-time approached, however, things didn't look good. Udinese were 2–0 down and heading for another defeat, until their young creative midfielder took control and inspired another fightback.

With a classy flick of his right foot, Bruno chipped a perfect pass over the Cagliari defence to Rodrigo Aguirre, who chested the ball down and scored. *2–1!*

Game on! Even when Cagliari scored again, Bruno still kept going, battling for every ball. He was an attacking midfielder on a goal-scoring mission. When the ball bounced out to the edge of the box, he got to it first and then fired a swerving shot into the top corner. *3–2!*

Gooooooooooooooooooooaaaaaaaaaaaaaaaaalllllllllllllll llllllllllll!!!!!!!!!!!!!!!!!!!!!!

It was a magnificent strike and he made it look so easy. At least he was ending his season on a high with a goal and an assist.

'That's more like it!' Bruno told himself as he ran back for the restart. 'Now I need to start playing like this every week.'

Consistently great performances, game after game – that was the next step for every young player, and Bruno would soon be twenty-one years old. His days as a rising star were running out. It was time for him to become the big game player his team needed him to be.

But how? There was no doubt that Bruno had the skill and the determination to reach the top, but he still had lots to learn if he was going to make the most of his tremendous talent. What did he need to do to add more goals and assists to his game? Tactics were a very important part of Italian football. The Serie A defences were so strong that attackers had to be really smart to break through and score. Luckily, Bruno had a legendary teammate who could help him with that.

'Try to always think at least one step ahead,' Toto told him as they did some extra training together. 'Where will the ball go next? How can I escape from my marker and find some space? Then once your chance arrives, stop thinking and just shoot!'

During preseason, Bruno spent hours practising making late runs into the box, and then smashing the ball past the keeper as quickly and powerfully as possible.

'Much better!' Toto encouraged his improving teammate. 'Now you just need to do that in matches!'

Bruno couldn't wait for the new Serie A season to begin, but when it did, sadly it was the same old story. Although he ran the Udinese midfield with his energy and passing, there was one very important thing missing: goals. Bruno created lots of chances for his teammates, but they just couldn't score. And when he decided to shoot, his wild strikes flew high and wide.

'Noooooo, what was that?' Bruno screamed up at the sky, kicking the air in frustration. Why couldn't he stay calm and finish like he did with Toto in training?

In the end, it took twenty-nine games for Bruno's first goal of the season to arrive. With Udinese 2–0 down against Roma with less than ten minutes to go, he raced forward as fast as he could to get into the box.

'Yes, I'm in space!'

The cross landed at Duván Zapata's feet instead, but the striker laid the ball back for Bruno to strike first time. This was it; the chance was too good to waste. He could hear Toto's words in his head:

'Stop thinking and just shoot!'

BANG! Bruno fired the ball through the last defender's legs and past the diving keeper. *2–1!*

Goooooooooooooooooooooaaaaaaaaaaaaaaaaalllllllllllllll llllllllllll!!!!!!!!!!!!!!!!!!!!

At last, he had scored! But there was no time for a big celebration; with a kiss of his wrist and an arm raised to the supporters, Bruno ran back for kick-off.

'Let's go, this game's not over yet!' he shouted to his teammates.

Unfortunately, however, Udinese couldn't grab an equaliser, and the defeat left them deep in the Serie A relegation battle. Surely they were too good to go down? But no, unless they started scoring goals and winning games, anything could happen...

Their next home game was against Napoli, the team chasing Juventus for the Serie A title. Tricky! To most people, a draw seemed like their best possible result, but Bruno wanted to win. Udinese needed all three points, not just one.

In the fourteenth minute, they were awarded a penalty and up Bruno stepped... to score – *1–0!*

'Come on, we can do this!' Bruno cried out, urging the fans in the Dacia Arena to make more noise.

Fifteen mad minutes later, however, the score was 1–1, and Bruno's second spot kick had been saved. Noooooo! But that mistake only made him more determined to win the match for Udinese. In the last minute of the first half, Bruno made another lung-busting, late run into the box, just like Toto had taught him.

'Yes!' he called out for the ball – he was totally unmarked!

Duván's cross was too deep for a header, so in a flash of quick-thinking, Bruno turned to Plan B. He backed away, swivelled his body around, and went for an overhead kick instead. BANG! His right foot connected with the ball beautifully and it flew past the Napoli defenders and into the net. *2–1!*

Goooooooooooooooooooooaaaaaaaaaaaaaaaallllllllllllllll llllllllllll!!!!!!!!!!!!!!!!!!

And what a goal it was, a moment of pure magic right when his team needed it most! At last, Bruno was becoming the big game player he had always wanted to be. As the Udinese fans cheered and cheered, he pumped his fists and leapt high into the air. There was no greater feeling than being a football hero.

CHAPTER 11

PORTUGAL'S NEXT STAR PLAYMAKER PART 1

After helping to rescue his club from relegation, Bruno took a well-deserved holiday with Ana and then switched his focus to his country. Fortunately, playing in Italy hadn't affected his international career so far. He had progressed rapidly through the Portugal youth teams, from the Under-19s to the Under-20s, and then to the Under-21s. He was part of a new golden generation – alongside the likes of Bernardo Silva, João Cancelo, Renato Sanches, Gonçalo Guedes and André Silva – and the coach, Rui Jorge, had even chosen him to be the captain. What an honour it was to wear the armband, and now, things were about to get even better because Bruno was off to play at the Olympics!

He couldn't wait to represent his country in Rio de Janeiro, Brazil, especially after watching the Portugal senior team beat France in the Euro 2016 final only one month earlier. What a night! Bruno had been at a training camp with Udinese at the time, with two French teammates, Thomas Heurtaux and Cyril Théréau. While everyone else sat together in front of a big TV screen, Bruno had watched most of the match alone in his room. France were the favourites, so it was probably for the best because everyone knew what a bad loser he could be. But as soon as Eder scored the winner in extra-time, Bruno sprinted down the corridor to join the others, screaming at the top of his voice.

Portugal! Portugal! Portugal!

As he watched his hero Cristiano Ronaldo lift the Euro 2016 trophy in Paris, Bruno felt proud and also inspired. 'What a summer it would be if we can bring back the Gold Medal too!' he said to his friend and Olympic teammate Gonçalo Paciência. And if they played really well, maybe they might soon get a call-up to the senior squad too, like Renato, who had just won the Best Young Player award at the Euros.

In the world of football, the Olympics wasn't quite as famous as the Euros or the World Cup, but it was still a major competition and a really exciting event to be a part of, alongside the best athletes from all over the world. Before the tournament began, Bruno looked back at the list of previous winners of the Gold Medal for men's football:

2000 – Samuel Eto'o's Cameroon, who beat Xavi's Spain in a penalty shoot-out

2004 – Argentina, with Carlos Tevez and Javier Saviola in attack

2008 – Argentina again, with an even more amazing team featuring Lionel Messi, Sergio Agüero and Ángel Di María!

2012 – Mexico, who beat Neymar Jr's Brazil in the final.

And what about 2016 – could it be a perfect year for Portugal? That was the plan! Okay, so they didn't have a world-class superstar like Cristiano Ronaldo in their team, or a lot of Bruno's best mates from the Under-21s, but there was still plenty of talent in the

Olympic squad. They showed it by beating Argentina 2–0 in their opening game. Gonçalo scored the first and super sub Pité scored the second, but who set up both goals? Bruno, of course, Portugal's next star playmaker!

The coach had put him on the left side of the midfield, but really he was everywhere, creating chance after chance with his clever movement and passing. Right foot, left foot, short or long – he could do it all, and Bruno was at it again three days later, leading Portugal to a 2–1 win over Honduras.

'Quarter-finals, here we come!' he celebrated with Gonçalo at the final whistle.

With the team already through to the knockout stage, Bruno was left on the bench for the final group game against Algeria. As always, he was desperate to come on, but Portugal needed to protect their star playmaker ahead of their big quarter-final against Germany.

Germany's side was packed with brilliant young players – Niklas Süle in defence, Leon Goretzka in midfield, and Julian Brandt and Serge Gnabry on the wings. Wow! It was going to be the toughest test yet for Bruno and his Portugal teammates.

For the first forty-five minutes, the score stayed 0–0, but just before half-time, Gnabry gave Germany the lead. It was a crushing blow for the Portugal players, and after that, they had no choice but to push forward on the attack. Bruno had several shooting opportunities but sadly he couldn't hit the target, and neither could any of his teammates. Germany, meanwhile, were clinical on the counter-attack and by the final whistle, they had won 4–0.

'Nooooooo!' Despite his best efforts, the Olympics were over for Bruno. Like every defeat, it hurt, but he was determined to learn from the experience. They had been beaten by a better team, so how could they come back stronger and win next time? After a few days, the disappointment began to fade, and Bruno could look ahead to his international future. First, he would lead Portugal to victory in the 2017 Under-21 Euros, and then the next step would be to join his hero Cristiano in the national senior squad.

CHAPTER 12

SAMPDORIA'S NEW NUMBER 10

Bruno's busy summer continued as soon as he got back to Italy. Just five days after playing for Portugal in the Olympic quarter-finals, he left Udinese to sign for another Serie A club – Sampdoria.

For Bruno, it felt like the right time to move on. He wanted to win trophies, and unfortunately, that didn't look likely at Udinese anymore. 'I've reached the end of the road,' he had announced at the end of the previous season. 'I think this is the right time for a step up in quality.'

That was a bold statement for a twenty-one-year-old to make, especially one who had only scored ten Serie A goals in eighty-six games. But as always, Bruno believed in himself and his ability. He felt ready to become a star for a bigger and better team.

There were lots of transfer rumours about a return to one of Portugal's top teams, but in the end, Bruno decided to stay in Italy and join Sampdoria instead. Although they had only finished two places above Udinese the previous season, the club had ambitious plans for the future. Under new manager Marco Giampaolo, Sampdoria were building an exciting young team. They had already bought defender Milan Škriniar, midfielders Lucas Torreira and Dennis Praet, and striker Patrik Schick, and now they would have Bruno too, pulling the strings in the playmaker role. At £6 million, he was the club's most expensive summer signing and so the pressure was already on for him to perform well, even before he chose to become Sampdoria's new Number 10.

It was the shirt that club legend Roberto Mancini had worn for fifteen years, including during the 1990–91 season when Sampdoria had won their one and only Serie A title. Since then, a long list of players had tried to live up to that famous Number 10 shirt

– Ariel Ortega, Francesco Flachi, Giampaolo Pazzini, Maxi López – but never with the same success. But was Bruno about to change all that?

'It's an honour to have the 10,' he told the local journalists. 'Does it weigh on me? No, I like challenges.'

As a playmaker, Bruno knew that a lot would depend on developing a good understanding with Sampdoria's two main strikers. He had played with Luis Muriel before at Udinese, so they knew each other's styles, while Fabio Quagliarella was one of Serie A's top finishers. Like Bruno's old friend Toto, if Fabio got a chance in front of goal, nine times out of ten, he scored. He just needed talented teammates who could create lots of chances for him.

'That's going to be me!' Bruno told himself with total confidence.

Although he began the new season on the bench, game after game, he got to play more and more minutes. Now, he just needed to show his manager that he was ready to step up into the starting line-up...

With Sampdoria 1–0 down away at Cagliari, Bruno came on and made an instant impact. As his team attacked up the left wing, he moved into the big open space on the right.

'Yes!' he called out for the ball.

When at last, the pass arrived, Bruno took his time and kept his cool. One touch to control, then a powerful shot past the keeper.

Goooooooooooooooooooooaaaaaaaaaaaaaaaaaalllllllllllllll llllllllllllll!!!!!!!!!!!!!!!!!!!!!

Yes, 1–1 – Sampdoria's new Number 10 was making a name for himself already! Bruno slid towards the corner flag on his knees, and he was soon surrounded by celebrating teammates.

'What a super sub!' Luis cheered.

Bruno was delighted with his goal, and after a few more moments of magic like that, hopefully he wouldn't be on the bench for much longer. A week later, he came on with Sampdoria in the same situation – 1–0 down against Palermo and struggling. It was time for him to save the day again.

'Yes!' Bruno called out as he raced into the Palermo penalty area unmarked. Luis spotted his run and crossed the ball in from the right, but as he slid in at the back post and stretched out his right leg, Bruno could only poke it wide.

'Unlucky, keep going!' Giampaolo shouted on the touchline.

As the minutes ticked by, it looked like Sampdoria were going to lose again, but no, Bruno wasn't going to let that happen. He ran and ran, trying everything to score, even another overhead kick like the one against Napoli. This time, though, the ball flew high over the bar.

'Ahhhhhhhhhhh!' the Sampdoria supporters groaned in disappointment.

But still, Bruno didn't give up, and his strong character shone through. With seconds to go, a Palermo defender headed the ball away to the edge of the box, where it bounced up beautifully for Bruno to strike first time. BANG! It was in the back of the net before the keeper could even react.

Gooooooooooooooooooooaaaaaaaaaaaaaaaaalllllllllllllll llllllllllll!!!!!!!!!!!!!!!!!!!!

Bruno had done it; he had saved the day for Sampdoria, just in time!

'Yes, you hero!' his teammates shouted, hugging him tightly.

Surely, now he deserved a spot in the starting line-up? Yes, and with Bruno on the ball all game long, Sampdoria soon became a much better team. With his intelligent passing and movement, he helped to link everything together.

Early on in the big local derby against Genoa, Bruno popped up on the right wing to fire a low cross into Fabio, who slid the ball across to Luis. *1–0!*

Just before half-time against Inter Milan, Bruno got the ball in the middle, skipped past one defender, and then slipped a killer pass through to Karol Linetty, who set up Fabio to score the winner. *1–0!*

Bruno was now just too brilliant to leave out. When Giampaolo put him on the bench against bottom-of-the-league Crotone, Sampdoria went 1–0 down. So, on he came in the second half to change the game and grab the equaliser.

'Yes, I knew you'd save us!' Lucas yelled, throwing his arms around Bruno.

Although he wasn't yet the complete, consistent big

game player that he wanted to become, Bruno could feel himself getting closer and closer to that target. His final ball had improved, and so had his decision-making, which meant more goals and more assists. At his best, he was now capable of winning matches almost on his own, as poor Pescara found out when they arrived at the Stadio Luigi Ferraris.

Luis dribbled into the box and picked out Bruno, who was waiting near the penalty spot. *1–0!*

From wide on the right, Bruno looked up and curled in a dangerous cross, which Fabio met with a diving header. *2–1!*

Ten minutes later, Bruno received the ball with his back to goal, but in a flash, he spun around and threaded an unbelievable pass through to Patrik. *3–1!*

'You're a genius!' the striker shouted as they hugged each other.

At last, wearing Sampdoria's Number 10 shirt, Bruno was starting to make the most of his tremendous creative talent. He was now a joy to watch, a joy to play with, and an absolute nightmare to play against.

CHAPTER 13

PORTUGAL'S NEXT STAR PLAYMAKER PART 2

Portugal's best young attackers and tallest defenders were all up in the Germany penalty area, waiting for the corner. Well, all except one.

'Yes!' Bruno called out to the taker, João Carvalho, as he made a late run towards the edge of the box. With no opponent anywhere near him, it was time to test out the set piece they'd practised in training.

João floated the ball over to his captain, who watched it carefully, all the way onto his right boot. BANG! Bruno struck it on the volley, and it swerved through the crowded box, before dipping down into the bottom corner. *1–0!*

Goooooooooooooooaaaaaaaaaallllllllllllllllllllllll!!!!!!!!!!

While the German players stood around in shock, Bruno raced over to the Portugal bench with his arms out wide and a huge smile on his face. What a strike! Their clever set-piece routine had worked perfectly, thanks to his stunning technique. Yes, it was only a friendly match, but revenge was still sweet after the Olympic quarter-finals. Plus, they were putting out a strong statement ahead of the main event that summer.

'Come on, we can win the Euros!' Bruno urged his Under-21 teammates on.

The Portugal squad that travelled to the tournament in Poland was packed with high-quality players: João Cancelo, Rúben Neves, Renato Sanches, Gonçalo Guedes, Daniel Podence, Diogo Jota… and of course, Bruno, who was proud to be the team leader.

'Right, is everyone ready for this?' he called out in the dressing room before their first game against Serbia.

They would have to be at their best from the start because there were only twelve national teams in the tournament and only the top four would go through to the semi-finals. That meant every match was a must-win, and any mistakes would be extra costly.

'YEAH!' Bruno's teammates responded with passion.

Serbia were strong, well-organised opponents, but Portugal's class shone through in the end as they scored two great team goals.

Late in the first half, Bruno fed the ball forward to Diogo, who picked out Daniel as he burst into the box. His cross was blocked by the keeper but Gonçalo was there to head home the rebound. *1–0!*

Then, late in the second half, Renato chipped a clever pass through to Bruno, who controlled the ball brilliantly on the run and then flicked it past the keeper. *2–0!*

Goooooooooooooooooooooaaaaaaaaaaaaaaaaallllllllllllll llllllllllllll!!!!!!!!!!!!!!!!!!!!!

'Thanks, mate!' Bruno shouted, rushing over to Renato, and lifting him high into the air.

So far, so good – Portugal were off to a winning start, but next up they faced their local rivals, Spain. Only one of them could finish top of Group B and secure a place in the semi-finals, but which would it be?

'Let the battle begin!' Bruno roared before kick-off.

It turned out to be an exciting, end-to-end game,

with plenty of chances for both teams, but it was Spain who made the most of their big moments. In the tenth minute, Daniel hit the post for Portugal, and shortly afterwards, Saúl Ñíguez dribbled up the other end and scored.

'Come on, concentrate!' Bruno cried out, flinging his arms up in frustration.

Rúben, Renato, and Bruno all had chances to equalise early in the second half, but their shots went high, wide, or straight at the keeper. Then in the sixty-fifth minute, Spain broke away on the counter-attack and scored again.

'There were four of you and only two of them!' Bruno wanted to shout and blame his defenders, but as the captain, he needed to stay calm and lead.

Portugal did eventually pull a goal back, thanks to a screamer from Bruma, but sadly the crucial next goal went to Spain instead. A 3–1 score – game over, and tournament over for Bruno and his teammates?

No, not quite yet. There was still one semi-final spot left for the best second-placed team, so Portugal just had to win their last group game against Macedonia by as many goals as possible, and then hope for the best. They would have to do it without their captain, however, because Bruno had been booked in both games.

'Come on, keep attacking!' he cheered his teammates on from the sidelines as Portugal took the lead in only the second minute.

By the final whistle, they had scored three more, but unfortunately, they had conceded two more too. That left them with a goal difference of +2 across all three games, but guess who finished above them on +4? Their old rivals, Germany.

'No, not them again!' Bruno groaned. First, they had knocked his team out of the Olympics and now they had dashed his Euro dreams as well.

Luckily, the doom and gloom didn't last for too long, though. That disappointing defeat to Spain turned out to be Bruno's last match for the Under-21s because a month later, he got his first call-up to the Portugal senior squad!

'Congratulations, you've earned it,' his Under-21s coach Rui Jorge told him with a smile. 'I guess I'll need to find a new captain now…'

Another of Bruno's dreams was about to come true! Although he didn't get to play in any of the 2018 World Cup qualifiers against the Faroe Islands, Hungary, Andorra and Switzerland, it was still an amazing experience to train with the established stars of the national team: Rui Patrício, Ricardo Quaresma, Pepe, Nani, and two of his ultimate football heroes, João Moutinho and Cristiano Ronaldo.

'I don't know what I'm going to say to those guys,' Bruno said nervously to Ana as he prepared to join up with the squad.

She laughed at her husband. 'Just say hello, like a normal person!'

At first, Bruno was happy to learn and wait his turn, but as the games went by, he grew more and more desperate to make his international debut. At last, the big day arrived on 10 November 2017, when Fernando Santos decided to rest a lot of his senior players for a friendly match against Saudi Arabia. And once Portugal had taken a comfortable 2–0 lead early in the second half, their coach made a triple substitution, bringing on Edgar Ié, Gelson Martins…

and Bruno!

Proudly wearing the Number 8 shirt often worn by Moutinho, Bruno raced onto the pitch and straight into the action. With one of his first touches as a Portugal player, he hit a swerving shot from over thirty yards out. Why not? It wasn't one of his best strikes, but he was off to a confident start for his country.

CHAPTER 14

SIGNING FOR SPORTING

As he stepped out onto the pitch that day to make his senior Portugal debut, Bruno was no longer a Sampdoria player. After five years in Italy, he had returned home to join Sporting Lisbon and fight for the Primeira Liga title.

Sporting Lisbon had been keeping a close eye on Bruno ever since his first breakthrough season at Udinese, but it was only in 2017 that they finally decided to make their move. The key moment came when the Sporting head coach Jorge Jesus and the club's sporting director André Geraldes went along to watch Bruno play for the Portugal Under-21s against Norway. Despite being the team captain, he only came on at half-time, but that still left plenty of time to change the game and change the minds of the Sporting men in the stadium.

'Yes, over here – I'm free!'

As soon as the second half kicked off, Bruno was calling for the ball and controlling the game with his clever passing and movement. He was everywhere – on the left, then on the right, dropping deep, then flying forward; and he was involved in everything – taking free kicks, corners, and powerful shots from all over the place. His ideas didn't always work out, but he had the confidence to keep trying until one of them did. And with their leader on the pitch, his Portugal teammates seemed to raise their play to the next level.

'Wow, he could be a real gamechanger for us,' Jesus and Geraldes agreed.

People in Portugal had always known that Bruno was a talented playmaker, but thanks to his time in Italy, he was now more mature and better at making decisions on the pitch. He had learnt when to speed things up with a moment of quick thinking, but also when to slow down and take his time on the ball. He could control a game and get the best out of the teammates around him too. Yes, Bruno was exactly the positive midfield maestro that Sporting so badly needed.

Luís Figo, João Moutinho, Cristiano Ronaldo – the club had produced so many brilliant players in the past, but it was now fifteen years since they had last won the Primeira Liga title, and three years since they had won any major trophy at all. They were falling further and further behind Porto and Benfica at the top, and that decline had to stop. But how?

Well, first of all, Sporting needed to be stronger at the back, so they signed defenders Fábio Coentrão from Real Madrid and Jérémy Mathieu from Barcelona. Great work! The next part of the plan was to be more creative in attack. William Carvalho and Adrien Silva could do all the defensive work in midfield, but what they needed was someone with skill and vision who could push the team forward and set up lots of chances for Bas Dost, their tall target man up front. That missing link was Bruno! Eventually, Sampdoria agreed to sell him for €8.5 million, and he became Sporting's second most expensive player ever.

But that was nothing compared to the buy-out clause in Bruno's new contract. If another club wanted to sign him now, they would have to pay a whopping €100 million! Wow, that was the highest fee in the history of Portuguese football – but Bruno didn't let it bother him as he posed for photos in the club's green-and-white-striped shirt.

Although the Number 10 shirt was available, this time he chose the Number 8 instead because that was his birthday, and it was also the number that so many of his heroes had worn – Moutinho, Iniesta, and even his dad during his early playing days.

'Right, let's start winning some trophies!' Bruno told his new teammates with a smile. He was happy to be home and playing in Portugal again, but he was still as ambitious as ever.

And still incredibly confident too. Just eighteen minutes into his league debut against Aves, Bruno chested the ball down on the edge of the box, twisted his way past his marker and fired a shot just wide of the post. So close to the perfect start! But it didn't

matter because Sporting still won the match, and
Bruno's first goal for the club would turn out to be
even better.

In the third minute of his third match, against
Vitória Guimarães, Bruno received the ball in the
middle of the pitch, spun quickly and dribbled forward
into space. He thought about passing, but as the
opposition's defenders backed away, he decided to go
for goal instead. Why not? He was over thirty yards
out, but he had scored from that distance many times
before. So, with a swing of his right leg, he sent the
ball swerving into the top corner at top speed. *1–0!*

*Goooooooooooooooooooooaaaaaaaaaaaaaaaalllllllllllllll
lllllllllll!!!!!!!!!!!!!!!!!!!*

The Guimarães keeper couldn't believe what
had just happened, and neither could the Sporting
supporters. But Bruno's teammates weren't surprised
at all; they saw what he could do in training every
day. As he leapt up and punched the air, they came
rushing over, one by one, to celebrate with him.

'What a worldie!' Gelson Martins cried out as he
threw his arms around him.

With his confidence up, Bruno kept attacking and in the second half, he scored again. This time, he dribbled all the way from the centre circle, and when no-one tried to tackle him, he decided to shoot from even further out. *BANG!* The ball flew past the diving keeper and into the bottom corner. *4–0!*

Goooooooooooooooooooaaaaaaaaaaaaaaaaalllllllllllllll llllllllllll!!!!!!!!!!!!!!!!!!!

Two wondergoals in one game – Bruno was starting his Sporting career in style! He raced over to the cheering supporters and stood in front of them, pumping his fists with passion. Their new hero had arrived.

'It's great to have you here!' Gelson yelled, jumping on his back.

'It's great to be here!' Bruno replied with a big grin on his face.

After that, the goals kept coming:

A curling free kick against Estoril,

A cheeky chip over the keeper against Feirense,

And then another long-range rocket against Tondela.

'Wow, who is this guy?' football fans all over Portugal were wondering. 'He's incredible!'

What a wise move it had been to return to Portugal! With five super-strikes in his first six games, Bruno was already on fire.

CHAPTER 15

TROPHY TIME AT LAST!

'Come on!' Bruno shouted joyfully as the Sporting players celebrated yet another victory. After seventeen games, they still hadn't lost a single match in the Primeira Liga and they were only two points behind Porto at the top of the table. 'Let's keep winning!'

The signings of Jérémy and Fabio had certainly helped to improve the Sporting defence, but it was Bruno who was making the biggest difference. Whether the manager asked him to play as a Number 8 in midfield or further forward as a Number 10, he moved around the pitch with freedom and confidence, connecting everything together for his team. He really was 'The New Iniesta' now! These days, Bruno didn't ever 'drift through games', as his old Udinese teammate Toto had once said; now, he was dominating every single one, scoring seven goals himself and setting up seven more for his teammates.

Four of those assists had come in an amazing forty-minute spell against Marítimo, where:

Bruno spun away from his marker and slipped a beautiful pass through to Bryan Ruíz. *2–0!*

He burst into the box and then unselfishly squared the ball to Bas for a tap-in. *3–0!*

The Marítimo keeper saved his powerful strike but Bas was there to head home. *4–0!*

In injury time, he had another shot saved, and this time the rebound fell to Marcos Acuña. *5– 0!*

'Thanks, Bruno!' Bas said, giving him a big hug. 'What would we do without you?'

All for €8.5 million – what a bargain! Suddenly, Bruno's €100 million buy-out clause didn't seem so silly now. After only six months at the club, he had already become Sporting's most important player. All that was missing now was a trophy. He was desperate to finally win his first as a professional footballer; it was the main reason for his return to Portugal. Surely, this was going to be his season? Sporting were still in the race for the Primeira Liga title, and they were through to the semi-finals of both Portuguese cup competitions too. But there was one big club standing in their way: Porto.

The two teams met first in the League Cup semi-final at Sporting's José Alvalade Stadium. It was an entertaining match, but after ninety minutes, neither side had scored, which meant... penalties!

'I'll take one,' Bruno told his manager straight away, with full belief and zero doubt. Although Bas usually took them in matches, Bruno had scored one from the spot against Braga earlier in the season, and he was sure that he could do it again.

As he walked forward from the halfway line, all three penalties so far had been scored. However, he kept his cool under pressure, and with a slow, stuttering run-up, he sent Iker Casillas the wrong way.

Goooooooooooooooooooooaaaaaaaaaaaaaaaaalllllllllllllll llllllllllll!!!!!!!!!!!!!!!!!!!!!

'Come on!' Bruno roared as he punched the air

with joy and relief.

And he was soon celebrating again when their keeper Rui Patrício saved Héctor Herrera's penalty. Advantage to Sporting! The next few minutes were really nerve-wracking but eventually, Bryan stepped up and scored the winning spot-kick.

'Yes, yes, YES!' Bruno screamed out as he sprinted over to join in the big team celebrations. 'We're in the final!'

Sporting were the favourites to beat Vitória de Setúbal in the final, but after five minutes, they were already 1–0 down. Bruno's old Olympic teammate Gonçalo Paciência turned on the edge of the box and fired a shot into the bottom corner.

'Nooooo!' Bruno groaned as he watched the ball nestle in the net.

It was the worst possible start for Sporting, but at least they still had plenty of time to battle their way back into the game. In the second half, they attacked the Vitória goal again and again, until eventually they grabbed an equaliser. As usual, it all started with Bruno, who crossed a high ball in towards his tallest teammate.

'This is it – go on!' the Sporting fans urged, rising to their feet with excitement.

Somehow, however, the keeper saved Bas's header and Fabio's follow-up shot, and then saved Bas's second header too. Or did he?

'HANDBALL!' Bruno bellowed, pointing down at his arm. He was certain that Bas's header had been saved by the Vitória defender, not the keeper.

And he was right. After a long VAR check, a penalty was awarded and this time, Bas did beat the keeper. *1–1!*

Game on, and Sporting still had fifteen minutes left to go and win it. Bruno drifted into space at the back post and Seydou Doumbia floated a perfect pass towards him. This was it: his chance to be the cup-winning hero. As he chested the ball down, time seemed to stand still. Then, *BANG!* Bruno fired a low shot towards the far bottom corner... but it flew just past the post.

'Argghhh!' he snarled, turning away in anger.

What a chance to win it for Sporting – and Bruno had blown it! He would have to make it up to his teammates by scoring from the spot because it was time for another penalty shoot-out. This time, the keeper did dive the right way, but he still couldn't save Bruno's accurate strike.

Goooooooooooooooooooaaaaaaaaaaaaaaaaallllllllllllll llllllllllll!!!!!!!!!!!!!!!!!!

Job done; now, for the nervous wait...

After Tomás Podstawski's penalty struck the crossbar, up stepped William to win the League Cup for Sporting.

Hurraaaaaaaaay!

All the players sprinted after William, but it was Bruno who grabbed him first. 'You did it – we did it!' He felt so proud of his teammates and proud of himself too. He had returned to Portugal with the aim of winning trophies and look what he had achieved already, with his friends and family there in the stadium watching.

One by one, the Sporting heroes made their way up onto the balcony to collect their winner's medals. Then, finally, came the moment Bruno had been waiting years for... trophy time! He stood next to his captain, Rui, as he held the cup between his goalkeeping gloves and then lifted it high into the air.

Hurraaaaaaaaaaaaaaaaaaaaaaaay!

As a kid growing up in Maia, these were the moments that Bruno had dreamed of – the confetti, the champagne, the celebrations, with a medal around his neck and the trophy in his hands. This one would be the first of many, he hoped.

CHAPTER 16

SCARY TIMES FOR THE "SPORTING NINE"

Once the League Cup celebrations were over, Bruno and his Sporting teammates turned their attention back to the Primeira Liga. It was still really tight at the top, with only five points between Porto in first place and Benfica in third. Sporting's main target was to win the league, of course, but as long as they stayed second, the supporters would be satisfied. Dropping down to third, however, would be a total disaster because this season, only Portugal's top two teams could qualify for the Champions League.

At the beginning of February 2018, Sporting were still three points ahead of Benfica, but a month later, they slipped three points behind and down into the dreaded third place.

'It's not over yet – we can still overtake them again!' Bruno tried to lift his teammates with his positive mindset, but for the first time at Sporting, he was struggling with his own form too. The 2–1 defeat away at Porto was his sixth league game in a row without a goal or an assist.

Bruno was shining brightly in the Europa League with three goals against FC Astana, so why couldn't he do the same back home in Portugal? There was no obvious answer, but he was determined to try everything to turn things around and take Sporting back up to second. Against Paços de Ferreira, Bruno even won a rare header in the box, flicking the ball on for Bas. *1–0!*

'Come onnnnn!' Bruno roared in front of the fans as if he had scored the goal himself. Sporting had signed him to be their matchwinner and he was determined to do just that. A week later, they were losing 1–0 away at Belenenses, until Bruno got on the ball and got his team back in the game. With an-inch perfect, long diagonal pass, he set up Bas to score. *1–1!*

'Come on, we need to win this!' Bruno called out as his teammates congratulated him on his amazing assist. Five minutes later, he dribbled forward and fed the ball through to Gelson. *2–1!*

Game over? No, not at all. With twenty minutes to go, the match was tied at 3–3, but up stepped Bruno to score the winner from the penalty spot.

What a hero! Bruno was back to his best and he scored both goals to beat Portimonense. They were his tenth and eleventh goals of the Primeira Liga season, but more importantly, Sporting were now back up to joint-second place! And who were they playing at home the next week? Benfica!

It was the perfect opportunity for Sporting to secure a Champions League spot, but sadly they couldn't make the most of it. The match finished 0–0, which meant it all came down to the final day of the season. What drama! Benfica were at home against Moreirense, while Sporting were away at Marítimo.

At half-time, both games were tied – 0–0 and 1–1. Early in the second half, however, Benfica took the lead, which meant that Sporting had to find a winning goal from somewhere…

They tried and tried, but the best they could do
was a Bruno shot that sailed just over the crossbar.
Noooooo! And to make matters even worse, Marítimo
scored a last-minute winner. Bruno's heart sank as he
watched the ball roll over the goal line. His hopes of
playing in the Champions League had been crushed.

Oh well, at least Sporting had won the League
Cup that season and they still had the final of the
Portuguese Cup to play. But according to some
supporters, that wasn't enough.

'Boooooooooo!' they jeered as the players left the
pitch. They were furious because they felt like their
heroes had really let them down by losing to Marítimo.

Two days later, the Sporting players and coaches
were at the training ground when all of a sudden a
group of fifty hooded men forced their way into the
changing room and started attacking them, saying:

'We're going to hurt you! You don't deserve to wear
the shirt!'

At first, Bruno just stood there, frozen in shock and
fear. What was going on? Was his life in danger? And

what about his wife, Ana, and his young daughter, Matilde – were they in danger too?

Eventually, the attack ended, but by then, serious damage had been done. The horrible experience left everyone feeling very upset and scared, while Bas even needed treatment for a bad head injury. How could the club's own supporters do that to their players?

Bruno just wanted to escape from the training ground as quickly as possible. He told Ana to take Matilde to Porto for a while, but would life ever feel safe at Sporting again? He didn't think so – the club was in total chaos. Only six weeks earlier, the president had tried to suspend nineteen of the first-team players just because they lost 2– 0 to Atlético Madrid in the Europa League. What on earth was going on?!

After the awful attack at the training ground, it was hard for the Sporting players to focus on football, and they lost 2–1 in the Portuguese Cup final five days later. It was a sad way to end a very promising season, but now Bruno had some serious thinking to do. He really wasn't sure that he wanted to play for the club anymore, and he wasn't the only one. Rui and Daniel were the first of the 'Sporting Nine' to quit the team, and a few weeks later, another seven stars asked for their contracts to be cancelled, including Bas, William, Gelson… and Bruno.

Yes, although he had enjoyed a sensational first season at the club, he wasn't going to stay where he didn't feel safe. So, where next for the new Primeira Liga Player of the Year? Well, that decision would have to wait because, first, Bruno was off to play for Portugal at the 2018 World Cup!

CHAPTER 17

2018 WORLD CUP

Thanks to his star performances for Sporting, everyone in Portugal now knew who Bruno was. He was a gamechanger, a matchwinner, capable of killer passes and stunning strikes. And so, when the national team coach, Fernando Santos, selected his squad for the World Cup in Russia, there was his name on the final list of twenty-three, alongside his heroes Ronaldo and Moutinho:

BRUNO FERNANDES.

He couldn't believe it. At the age of twenty-three and with only four caps for his country, he was going to the World Cup! Even if he didn't get to play a single second, it would still be a dream come true.

But Bruno being Bruno, he didn't want to just sit on the bench. Yes, the Portugal squad was packed with amazing attacking midfielders – Gelson, Bernardo Silva, Adrien Silva, João Mário, Ricardo Quaresma, Manuel Fernandes – but he believed that he was one of the best and he was ready to prove it.

Bruno was desperate to play, and he had two pre-tournament friendlies left to try and impress his manager. He only came on for the last few minutes in the first one against Belgium, but he was in the starting line-up for the second against Algeria. He would be on the left wing, with Bernardo Silva on the right, and Gonçalo Guedes and Cristiano up front.

'Right, it's my time to shine!' Bruno thought positively as he walked out into the Estádio da Luz in Lisbon. He was determined to make the most of his opportunity, but what could he come up with?

An assist? Early on, Bruno slipped a beautiful pass through to Cristiano, who danced his way past two defenders and scored. But sadly, the linesman's flag was up – offside!

'Ohhhh!' Bruno groaned with his hands on his

head. So close to creating Portugal's first goal! Oh well, there was still plenty of time left.

'Great ball – keep them coming!' Cristiano encouraged him with a quick thumbs-up.

Bruno did as he was told, chipping another clever pass through to his captain, who forced the Algeria keeper into a good save. So close again! By then, Portugal were already 1–0 up, thanks to a goal from Gonçalo, but they wanted more…

A goal? As half-time approached, Portugal's attackers swapped positions. Cristiano moved out to the left wing and swung a dangerous cross into the middle for… Bruno! Although heading wasn't his greatest strength, he timed his jump perfectly, and powered the ball past the keeper. *2–0!*

Goooooooooooooooooooooaaaaaaaaaaaaaaaaaalllllllllllllll lllllllllllll!!!!!!!!!!!!!!!!!!!

What a time to score his first for his country! But despite his achievement, Bruno didn't get carried away with excitement. Instead, he jogged calmly over to Cristiano for a high-five and a hug. 'Thanks, what a cross!'

Job done! With that goal against Algeria, Bruno
had booked his place in Portugal's World Cup first
XI. Once in Russia for the tournament, Santos stuck
with the same attack for their first group game against
Spain, and they got off to the best possible start. In
only the fourth minute, Bruno headed José Fonte's
long ball down to Cristiano, who skipped his way into
the box and fooled the right-back, Nacho Fernández,
with a fancy stepover.

FOUL, PENALTY… 1–0!

'Come onnnnn!' Bruno cried out as he waited for
Cristiano to finish his special celebration, so that he
could give him a hug. Portugal were up and running
at the 2018 World Cup, but there turned out to be
many twists and turns to come:

Diego Costa used his strength and skill to make
space for the shot. *1–1!*

Cristiano went for goal from the edge of the area
and somehow the ball squirmed through David de
Gea's gloves. *2–1 to Portugal!*

Sergio Busquets headed the ball across goal for
Diego to slide it in. *2–2!*

Then three minutes later, Nacho made up for his earlier mistake by scoring a screamer. *3–2 to Spain!*

It was a stunning strike, but who was supposed to be marking him? Bruno, playing on the left of the Portugal midfield. He turned and raced over to try and block the shot, but it was too late. As he watched the ball bounce off the post and into the back of Rui's net, his heart sank. At the top level, even the tiniest mistakes could be really costly. Ten minutes later, Santos made his first substitution: on came João Mário and off went Bruno.

'Well played,' his manager said as he left the pitch, but Bruno couldn't help feeling disappointed with himself. He knew that he could play a lot better than that, but would he get another chance to prove it? It looked unlikely when Cristiano completed his hat-trick to give Portugal an important point. Maybe they were better off without him?

For Portugal's next match, against Morocco, Santos made one change to his starting line-up: João Mário in and Bruno out. Bruno did come on for the last twenty minutes, but despite his best efforts, he failed to make an impact for Portugal. One cross didn't quite reach Cristiano, one shot trickled a long wide, then another ballooned high over the bar. And that turned out to be it; the end of his first World Cup.

Portugal drew 1–1 with Iran, but Bruno didn't leave the bench.

Portugal lost 2–1 to Uruguay in the Round of 16, but again, Bruno didn't leave the bench.

He watched with frustration as Santos called for Ricardo, then André Silva, and then Manuel to get warmed up and ready for action instead. It was absolute agony for Bruno, but at least he was still young and still as strong a character as ever. There would be many more major international tournaments ahead for him: Euro 2020, the 2022 World Cup… and by then, he would have proved himself as one of Portugal's first-choice playmakers. He had no doubt about that.

CHAPTER 18

SPORTING SUPERSTAR

'It doesn't matter who is to blame, now it is over,' Bruno explained at the press conference. 'Sporting is opening a new page and I believe it will be very good.'

Less than a month ago, Bruno had cancelled his contract at Sporting, but after a change of heart, he was back there! Despite interest from English clubs Newcastle United and West Ham, he had decided to return to Sporting, where a lot had changed since the scary training ground attack. The club now had:

A new president, Frederico Varandas,

A new manager, Marcel Keizer,

A new captain, Nani,

And a new vice-captain, Bruno!

With more responsibility and a brand-new big-money contract, he couldn't wait to get started again. He had unfinished business, especially in the Primeira Liga and the Portuguese Cup.

'Come on, we've got trophies to win!' Bruno told his teammates.

Sadly, Rui, William, Daniel and Gelson had all already signed for new clubs, but Bas was back for the new season, and Sporting had just spent €6.5 million on an exciting young Brazilian winger called Raphinha. The line-up looked strong, and by the end of the opening game of the season, Bruno already had his first goal and assist, and Sporting had their first win.

'I'm so glad you're back!' Bas yelled out as they celebrated together. 'What would we do without you?'

Bruno was at the centre of everything, taking charge for Sporting whether he was wearing the captain's armband or not. He was always running and talking to his teammates, often at the same time.

'Flick it on, Bas!'

'Make the run, Raphinha!'

Bruno took all the corners for Sporting, some of the penalties, and when Nani moved to America to play in the MLS in February, all of the free kicks too. 'I've got this,' he told his teammates, and they trusted their leader completely. Thanks to hours of extra practice after training and studying videos of set-piece superstars like David Beckham and Dejan Stanković, Bruno was getting better and better at scoring from any distance and from any angle.

'Okay, that's enough for tonight,' his manager would often say, having had to go out on to the training ground and tell him. 'Save your energy for tomorrow's match!'

There was no stopping Sporting's new free-kick king. Away at Feirense, Bruno took one from the left and curled the ball up over the wall and into the corner.

Goooooooooooooooooooooaaaaaaaaaaaaaaaaaallllllllllllll llllllllllllll!!!!!!!!!!!!!!!!!!!!

In the next game against Braga, he took one from the right and sent the ball dipping and swerving past the keeper at his near post.

Goooooooooooooooooooooaaaaaaaaaaaaaaaaaallllllllllllll llllllllllllll!!!!!!!!!!!!!!!!!!!!

Bruno slid across the grass on his knees, pumping his fists at the Sporting supporters above. He had just equalled his previous best of eleven league goals, and there were still twelve more games to go. During his time in Italy, Bruno had been a deep-lying playmaker who averaged only four strikes a season, but at Sporting he had blossomed into a midfield goalscoring machine, as poor Belenenses were about to find out.

With sixty-five minutes played, Bruno's team were winning 3–1, but he wasn't satisfied because his name wasn't on the scoresheet. Yet. So far, all of his shots had been blocked, but as always, he had the confidence to keep trying until he got one right. In the end, Bruno's first goal of the game came from the penalty spot. Raphinha was so sure that his captain would score that he started celebrating even before he kicked the ball. He was right; with his trademark skip and a jump, Bruno sent the keeper the wrong way.

Goooooooooooooooooooaaaaaaaaaaaaaaaaaalllllllllllllll llllllllllll!!!!!!!!!!!!!!!!!!

'Finally!' he groaned as he high-fived his teammates. Uh-oh, the beast had been woken – Belenenses were really in trouble now! Five minutes later, Bruno calmly fired the ball into the net again, after a cutback from striker Luiz Phellype.

Goooooooooooooooooooooaaaaaaaaaaaaaaaalllllllllllllllll llllllllllll!!!!!!!!!!!!!!!!!!!!

'Thanks, mate!' he shouted, jumping into Luiz's arms.

Bruno had scored two goals in lots of matches for Sporting, but never three. Was this the day for his first-ever professional hat-trick? The Belenenses players were already waiting for the final whistle to blow, but there were still fifteen minutes to go...

'Yes!' Bruno yelled as he made another late run into the box. Out on the left wing, Marcos Acuña heard his captain's call and curled a high cross towards him. As the ball dropped, Bruno steadied himself and watched it all the way onto his boot. BANG! It wasn't one of his sweetest strikes, but it still landed in the net.

Gooooooooooooooooooooaaaaaaaaaaaaaaaalllllllllllllllll llllllllll!!!!!!!!!!!!!!!!!!!!

Hat-trick hero! Holding three fingers up, Bruno raced over to the Sporting fans and slid on his knees in front of them. What a season he was having – he made the Primeira Liga look so easy. That was his nineteenth league goal and his thirty-first across all competitions! He was the proud new owner of the record for the most goals scored by any Portuguese midfielder ever in a single season. Wow, and he had set up another seventeen goals for his teammates too! Was there a better attacking midfielder than Bruno anywhere in world football?

'No way!' The Sporting supporters believed that their superstar was the best, but they kept quiet because they were desperate to keep him at the club. Despite Bruno's brilliance, however, it was the same old story for Sporting in the Primeira Liga – a third place finish, behind Porto and the champions, Benfica. Nooooo, not again! Sadly, they just couldn't keep their good form going across a full thirty-four-game league season.

Knock-out cup competitions, however, were a different matter. There, Sporting excelled. With wins over Marítimo, Estoril Praia, Feirense, and Braga, they made it through to the League Cup final again. This

time, they faced Porto, but the outcome was the same
– PENALTIES!

They were such a nerve-wracking experience for
most players, but not for Bruno and Bas. They had
been in this position before and so the pressure didn't
bother them as they both stepped up and scored. 2–1
to Sporting! After a great save from their keeper Renan
Ribeiro, Nani made it 3–1, meaning Porto had to
score their next penalty, or it was all over. Felipe ran
up and… hit the crossbar!

'Yes, yes, YESSSSSSS!' Bruno screamed as he raced
over to celebrate with Renan and the rest of his
teammates. Sporting had won the League Cup for a
second year in a row! But the big question was could
they go on and win the cup double this time? Four
months later, Sporting and Porto would face each
other again, in the final of the Portuguese Cup.

CHAPTER 19

DOING THE DOUBLE

Bruno was desperate to win the Portuguese Cup this time. Despite all his great goals and superstar performances, he still hadn't forgotten about the sad end to the previous season – the awful training ground attack and then the shock defeat to Aves in the cup final a few days later. Although the Sporting players had agreed to go ahead with the game, their performance had been poor – sloppy at the back and wasteful in attack. So, Bruno was more determined than ever to lead Sporting back to the final in 2019 and lift that trophy at last.

GOAL! Bruno scored a long-range screamer against Loures.

GOAL! He finished in style after a one-two with Bas against Lusitano.

GOAL! He fired a right-foot rocket into the top corner against Rio Ave.

GOAL! He fired a right-foot rocket into the bottom corner against Feirense.

Four games, four great goals. 'Do you ever just score simple tap-ins?' his midfielder partner, Nemanja Gudelj, asked as they celebrated together.

Bruno smiled cheekily. 'No, why would I do that when I can score a beauty instead?'

With their superstar on fire, Sporting were through to another Portuguese Cup semi-final, but things were about to get a lot tougher. Their next opponents would be Benfica, the team at the top of the Primeira Liga table, who hadn't lost a match in months. That didn't bother Bruno, though; in fact, he was looking forward to the challenge.

'Hey, they might be the league leaders, but remember, we're the kings of the cups!' he told his teammates before kick-off.

In the first leg away at the Estadio da Luz, Sporting

were 2–0 down with ten minutes to go when Bruno placed the ball down for a free kick. It was a long way out, even for him, but somehow he managed to put enough power and curl on the ball to send it flying into the top corner.

Goooooooooooooooooooaaaaaaaaaaaaaaaaallllllllllllll llllllllllll!!!!!!!!!!!!!!!!!!!!

And most importantly, an away goal. Back at the Estádio José Alvalade, Sporting defended well, knowing that they just needed to score one goal to win it and reach the final. That sounded straightforward but when Bruno hit the crossbar with another fantastic free kick, the fans began to worry. Where was their winning goal going to come from?

Bruno, of course! From wide on the right wing, he faked to cross the ball in but instead, he cut inside, fooling the Benfica left-back. Now what? There were plenty of other Sporting players in the box, but Bruno only had one thing on his mind:

Goooooooooooooooooooaaaaaaaaaaaaaaaaallllllllllllll llllllllllll!!!!!!!!!!!!!!!!!!!!

What a strike, and with his weaker left foot too!

Bruno raced straight over to the Sporting supporters, buzzing with adrenaline and emotion. He had just scored his most important goal ever for the club.

Come onnnnnnn!

Twenty tense minutes later, the final whistle blew, and Bruno had done it; he had led Sporting back to the Portuguese Cup final. Now for the last step: lifting the trophy!

In the final itself, Bruno refused to be beaten. Even when Porto took the lead late in the first half, he urged his team to keep going and push forward. As Marcos dribbled up the left wing, Bruno drifted into space in his danger zone – the centre of the pitch, just outside the penalty area…

'Yes!' he called and when the pass arrived, he took one touch to control it and then fired a shot off a defender and into the net. *1–1!*

Goooooooooooooooooooooaaaaaaaaaaaaaaaaallllllllllllll llllllllllll!!!!!!!!!!!!!!!!!!

Despite the deflection, Sporting's captain was claiming it as his own. Bruno leapt into the air, with chest out and his fists pumping. What a hero! Then, as the TV cameras zoomed in on him, he put his hands over his ears – his special celebration for his daughter, Matilde – and blew kisses to her.

'Right, let's go on and win this now!' Bruno inspired his teammates, and in extra-time, Bas scored what looked to be the winner. But no, back came Porto with a last-minute header. 2–2! The final would be decided on penalties… again!

For once, Bas missed his spot-kick, but not Bruno. With Sporting 2–0 down, he stayed calm and sent the keeper the wrong way. Although he didn't celebrate or shout like he usually did, Bruno's goal seemed to lift the team spirit. Jérémy went next and scored, then Raphinha, and then Sebastián. It was now down to sudden death – which team would make the first mistake? Porto's Fernando Andrade struck his penalty hard and low… but Renan flew across his goal to make a supersave!

So, up walked Luiz with the chance to win it for Sporting.

'Go on, go on…' Bruno muttered under his breath on the halfway line. He could hardly bear to watch.

All their striker had to do was score! …And he did.

Yes, Sporting had won the Portuguese Cup! There were emotional scenes all over the pitch – Luiz sank to his knees next to the penalty spot, Renan lay sprawled on the grass, while Bruno ran over to the sidelines to celebrate with Nemanja.

'We did it, we did it!' they shouted joyfully as they rolled around on the grass together.

While Sporting hadn't won the Primeira Liga title, they had won both of Portugal's cup competitions in the same season. And this one was extra special for Bruno because as the captain, he got to lift the trophy first, fulfilling his childhood dreams. And boy, did he deserve it, after scoring in all seven of Sporting's cup games. What a leader he had become!

'Ready?' With his teammates all around him, Bruno held the cup in his hands and waited for the right moment to raise it high above his head.

Three, two, one…

'Hurraaaaaaaay!' the Sporting players shouted as confetti showered down on them. As Bruno cheered, he looked out across the stadium at the sea of green-

and-white shirts and flags, at the 20,000 supporters enjoying their team's success. There really was no greater feeling in the world.

CHAPTER 20

PORTUGAL'S NEW STAR PLAYER

By the summer of 2019, Bruno wasn't just starring for Sporting; he was starring for Portugal too. At last, he had broken into the national team because how could they leave out the two-time Primeira Liga Player of the Year and Europe's top-scoring midfielder?

'Put Bruno in the team!' the Portuguese football fans urged, and not only the ones who supported Sporting.

Santos, the manager, listened. Despite only playing a few minutes in the first four matches in UEFA's brand-new tournament, the Nations League, Bruno moved into the starting line-up for the semi-final against Switzerland in June 2019, at home in Portugal at

Porto's Estádio do Dragão. Could he help his country to win a second top international trophy to go with Euro 2016?

The pressure was on for Bruno to perform like he did for his club, but fortunately, he was surrounded by lots of familiar faces. He would be playing in midfield with his old Under-21 teammate, Rúben Neves, and his old Sporting teammate, William Carvalho. Then, ahead of him in attack would be his young Benfica opponent João Félix, and his World Cup teammates Bernardo and Cristiano. With that all-star line-up together on the same pitch, it was no surprise that Portugal made it through to the Nations League final with a 3–1 win.

'Now for the trophy!' Cristiano cheered as he celebrated yet another amazing hat-trick with the rest of the squad.

But while Cristiano was the captain and their greatest superstar, he was no longer Portugal's only stand-out player. There was a new exciting and talented generation coming through: defenders Rúben Dias and João Cancelo, forwards João Félix and

Gonçalo Guedes, and best of all, midfield magicians Bruno and Bernardo.

Like Bruno, Bernardo had made the brave decision to leave Portugal at a young age, moving to French football league club Monaco. And after three excellent seasons there, he had signed for Manchester City, where he had just won back-to-back Premier League titles.

'England is the place to be,' he kept telling Bruno. 'Come join me!'

Bruno and Bernardo were good friends off the pitch, and that helped them to form a fantastic partnership on it, for Portugal. They were both brilliant playmakers, and together in the same team, they were even better, like Portugal's own version of Iniesta and Xavi. Again and again, it was Bruno who launched the attacks against Switzerland, feeding the ball through to Bernardo, who then created chances for Cristiano. What a dream team!

The same thing happened again in the final against the Netherlands, only this time Portugal's two midfield playmakers were even more impressive. In the first half in particular, they were everywhere, dominating the game with their clever passing and movement.

Bernardo tapped a quick corner to Bruno, who crossed the ball onto Cristiano's head. *Saved!*

Bruno showed no fear of shooting from long distance. *Saved!*

Bruno escaped his marker with a chop-back and then played a glorious pass to Nélson Semedo with the outside of his right foot. *Olé!*

Bernardo passed it through to Bruno who blasted the ball over. *Missed!*

Bernardo laid the ball back to Bruno who curled a shot just over the crossbar. *So close!*

'Arghhhh!' Bruno put his hands to his face and then let out a groan of frustration. How many more good chances was he going to waste?

The Netherlands came out stronger in the second half, but in the sixtieth minute, at last a goal arrived for Portugal. Bernardo dribbled his way into the box and then cut the ball back to Gonçalo. *1–0!*

'Come on!' Cristiano cheered, high-fiving Bruno as they chased over to the corner to celebrate with

Gonçalo and Bernardo.

Now, Portugal just had to stay strong and hold on for the victory. After eighty-one minutes of tireless, box-to-box running, Bruno was replaced by João Moutinho.

'Well played, what a performance!' his old hero said with a smile as they high-fived.

Bruno sat down for a well-deserved rest on the bench, but before long, he was back on his feet and back out on the pitch to shake hands with his opponents and then celebrate with his teammates. It was all over, and Portugal were the winners of the first-ever UEFA Nations League!

'Bruno, get over here!' Cristiano called out, bringing all of his teammates together in a big group hug. 'Well done, we did it guys!'

'Come onnnnnnn!'

Soon, Bruno was standing up on the stage with a winner's medal around his neck, waiting for his captain to collect the trophy. As Cristiano carried it over, the other Portuguese players began to build up the tension and excitement:

Ohhhhhhhhhhhhhhhhhhhh...

Only once he was at the centre of the stage, in front of the Portuguese flag, did Cristiano finally lift the trophy to the sky.

…Hurraaaaaaaaaaaaaaaaaaaaaaay!

As the fireworks exploded and the confetti fell, Bruno threw both arms up in the air and let out a long passionate roar. He was so proud to represent his country and help bring joy to the nation. Although it was his fourteenth cap, it still felt like a dream to be playing for Portugal, and winning the UEFA Nations League was a moment and a feeling that he would never, ever forget.

Another top performance and another top trophy – what a perfect way to end the best season of Bruno's career by far. But what next for Portugal's new star player?

CHAPTER 21

MOVING TO MANCHESTER... EVENTUALLY!

As Bruno stood there on the stage celebrating his UEFA Nations League success with Portugal, the rumours were already flying about his future. Surely, he was now too good to stay at Sporting for another season? Even Cristiano had said so! According to the news stories, all of the biggest Premier League clubs were desperate to sign him:

Manchester United saw him as the missing piece, the magician who could help them win trophies again;

Manchester City were offering him the chance to team up with his friend Bernardo, Portugal's two best playmakers together;

Liverpool were looking for a creative midfielder

to link up with Mohamed Salah, Sadio Mané and Roberto Firmino;

And Tottenham wanted him to replace Christian Eriksen as their playmaker behind Harry Kane and Son Heung-min.

Apparently, they were all willing to pay a massive price too – some newspapers said €50 million, while others went as high as €70 million. Wow, Bruno really was a much-wanted midfielder now! Signing for a top Premier League team had been his dream since he was a young boy, but he wasn't going to get his hopes up until a deal had been done.

'I'm calm, I have a contract with Sporting, I'm in a big club,' he told the Portuguese journalists when they asked about his plans. 'I also have dreams I want to come true, but I do not know if it's going to be this year.'

Bruno was ready to take the next step and challenge for the top trophies – the big league titles and European cups. But he wasn't going to rush; he was still only twenty-four years old, and he had already played for five different clubs. So, he was happy to wait until the right offer came along, both for him and for Sporting.

Manchester United sent scouts to watch Bruno play, but they decided against signing him, despite what the Portuguese newspapers said. In fact, during the summer of 2019, Tottenham were the English team leading the race to sign him. Bruno and his agent, Jorge Mendes, met the Spurs manager, Mauricio Pochettino, to discuss the club's plans for the future, and they sounded really exciting. Tottenham had big ambitions to win lots of trophies, just like Bruno himself, and they were offering him the chance to play in the Premier League and in the Champions League as well.

'Okay, I'm ready to sign for Spurs,' Bruno told Mendes – but in the end, the move collapsed because of money. Tottenham offered €45 million, plus an extra €20 million if they won a major trophy, but the Sporting president Frederico Varandas said no. He wanted at least €55 million for his superstar straight away.

Sadly, there was no second offer from Spurs, or any

bids from other big clubs, but Bruno didn't lose hope or complain. Instead, he stayed positive and just got on with preparing for the new season at Sporting. He was still the club captain, after all.

'Until the last day I am here, I will always do my best,' he told the journalists, and he worked hard to keep his word.

GOALS! He danced his way through the Braga defence, before blasting a shot past the keeper.

ASSISTS! He set up all three Sporting goals away at Portimonense.

GOALS AND ASSISTS! He played a part in all four goals to lead his team past PSV Eindhoven in the Europa League. Including:

With a flick of his right foot, Bruno lifted the ball into the box for Luiz to head in. *1–0!*

Five minutes later, he dribbled forward and fired a low, skidding strike into the bottom corner. *2–0!*

He curled a high corner towards the back post, where Jérémy slid in to score. *3–0!*

From the penalty spot, he sent the keeper the wrong way. *4–0!*

What a superstar! When the transfer window opened again in January, Bruno was up to fifteen goals and fourteen assists already, in only twenty-eight games. Surely, he was worth €55 million now, if not more?

It was too late for Tottenham, who had signed Tanguy Ndombele from Lyon instead, but what about Manchester United?

Although they had said no in the summer, things were different now because their season was in danger of falling apart. After disappointing defeats to Arsenal, Liverpool, and Burnley, they had dropped down to fifth in the Premier League table. Nooooooo! A big club like Manchester United couldn't afford to miss out on qualifying for the Champions League again. They had to do something to get back into the Top Four, but what?

The team had problems at the back and in attack, but everyone agreed that what they needed most was a new midfielder playmaker. Since Paul Pogba had picked up an ankle injury in September, Manchester United had been struggling to create enough chances

for their forwards. The manager Ole Gunnar Solskjær
had tried playing Jesse Lingard, Juan Mata, and
Andreas Pereira as a Number 10, but none of them
was quite right for the role. What was missing was an
all-action midfielder with energy, skill, vision, and goals
– what was missing, in other words, was... Bruno!

Bruno just hoped that the transfer rumours were
true this time. If they were, he would get the chance
to achieve two of his football dreams at the same time:

1)   To play in the Premier League

and

2)   To play for Manchester United!

He had loved the club ever since the age of eight,
when Sir Alex Ferguson signed Cristiano from
Sporting and helped him become a superstar. Now,
seventeen years later, was Bruno about to make
exactly the same move and follow in his hero's
footsteps? He asked Cristiano for his advice and spoke
to his former Sporting teammate Nani too. Both of
them said the same thing: 'Go on, you've got to sign
for United!'

And so did Ricardo, Bruno's older brother.

He lived in London now, where he worked as a hospital assistant, but he didn't mind travelling up to Manchester to enjoy free tickets at Old Trafford. 'I'll be able to watch you play every week,' he said excitedly. 'Get ready for lots of criticism, just like when we were young!'

It took a few more weeks of negotiating, but eventually, on 29 January 2020, the deal was done for €80 million: €55 million, plus an extra €25 million depending on how many top trophies he helped them win. At last, the news was official:

'Manchester United is delighted to announce it has reached an agreement with Sporting Clube de Portugal for the transfer of Bruno Fernandes.'

Hurray! The United fans were delighted; after months of waiting and hoping, they finally had the midfield magician they wanted. Sporting, however, had lost their superstar and leader. 'For the two-and-a-half years I was here, I can only thank them for everything,' Bruno said in an emotional goodbye to everyone at the club. 'I hope that you stay with good memories of me, and I will always take you in my heart.'

Bruno was about to become a Manchester United player – unbelievable, those words still sounded too good to be true! But no, it was really happening; all his hard work in Portugal and Italy had paid off because he had just signed for one of the biggest clubs in the world. As he posed for his first photos in the club's famous red shirt, he couldn't help smiling, and mentioning his hero, of course:

'Now I want to write my history, different to Cristiano because he is the best player in the world,' Bruno said. 'I want to give my best to write my name in the history of Manchester United.'

CHAPTER 22

AN INSTANT IMPACT AT OLD TRAFFORD

'Fernandes will need time to adapt – remember Ronaldo's first season here? He was rubbish!'

'Yeah, he'll find the Premier League a lot more challenging than playing in Portugal, that's for sure!'

Manchester United's new signing was arriving at Old Trafford halfway through the 2019–20 season, and so the supporters tried not to expect too much too soon. Bruno himself, however, was determined to settle in quickly and find his best form straight away. After one training session, he was already telling his new teammates what to do.

'Go forward – don't be afraid!' Bruno called out to the right-back Aaron Wan-Bissaka.

'Yes, pass it to me!'

'Come on, we've got to move the ball quicker!'

As he watched from the sidelines, Solskjær smiled. What a signing Bruno was going to be! He was exactly what the team needed – a player with lots of personality and a brilliant football brain. Although Manchester United's next match was only two days away, the manager decided to put him straight into the starting line-up.

'Just be your brilliant self out there tonight, okay?'

'Thanks, I'll do my best, boss!'

Bruno tried to stay calm and focused as he walked out onto the pitch at Old Trafford for the first time, but it wasn't easy. Wow, what an atmosphere! And was that his name he could hear the fans already chanting?

Bruno had made the brave decision to wear the Number 18, the shirt that used to belong to Manchester United's legendary midfielder Paul Scholes. 'Why not?' he thought to himself. 'I'm already under a lot of pressure to perform, so a little bit more won't make any difference.' Scholes was another of his football heroes, so for Bruno it was an honour to wear the same shirt, as well as a responsibility.

Right, it was time to kick off his Manchester United career.

'Yes!' he called for the ball straight away.

Bruno kept his first few touches nice and simple, especially as he was playing against Wolves, who had his Portugal teammates João and Rúben in midfield. But Bruno's style was to be positive with the ball. He wanted to play forward, not sideways, or backwards, and so as the game went on, he took more and more risks.

PING! He played a long diagonal pass towards Anthony Martial, but the defender got there first.

NUTMEG! He poked the ball through Matt Doherty's legs for Daniel James to chase after.

BANG! He hit a powerful, long-range shot that swerved just wide of Rui Patrício's post.

CURL! He fired a free kick towards the top corner, but Rui made the save.

The result against Wolves was 0–0 – oh well, it wasn't the dream debut that Bruno had been hoping for, but it was a solid first performance, with flashes of the brilliance to come…

Just before half-time in Manchester United's next home match against Watford, Bruno raced onto Daniel's through-ball, but as he knocked it past the keeper, his legs were clipped. *PENALTY!*

Bruno picked himself up, grabbed the ball, and with his usual skip and jump, he sent the keeper the wrong way. *1–0!*

Gooooooooooooooooooooaaaaaaaaaaaaaaaaaalllllllllllllll llllllllllllll!!!!!!!!!!!!!!!!!!!!

Hurray, he was off the mark at Manchester United and making a difference already! Bruno slid towards the corner flag on his knees with his hands over his ears. New club, same old celebration.

'Yes, my friend!' Fred cheered as he chased after him.

Bruno's big day soon got even better, as he helped set up both of United's second-half goals as well. First, he slipped a perfect pass through to Anthony who had his first shot saved, but scored the rebound. Then, twenty minutes later, Mason Greenwood broke away on the counter-attack, played a one-two with Bruno, and finished in style. *3–0!*

Bruno didn't need a season to settle in; he was ready to become a United hero straight away!

'I'm very excited to have him here,' Solskjær said after the game. 'He has come in and given everyone a boost.'

With his box-to-box energy and positivity, Bruno was bringing out the best in everyone around him. Whenever he was on the pitch, United looked faster, stronger, hungrier, and much more likely to score. His key contributions continued away at Everton, when he got the ball in his danger zone: the centre of the pitch, just outside the penalty area... BANG! Bruno hit the shot first time and it swerved and dipped under the diving keeper. *1–1!*

Goooooooooooooooooooaaaaaaaaaaaaaaaallllllllllllll llllllllllll!!!!!!!!!!!!!!!!!!

'Come on!' Bruno was making the Premier League look just as easy as the Primeira Liga. He was brimming with confidence and it was inspiring his teammates too.

Next up: the Manchester derby – United vs City, and Bruno vs Bernardo. In the days leading up to the big match, they messaged each other, both believing their team was going to win. But at home at Old Trafford, it was Bruno who came out on top.

In the first half, United were playing well but they were missing that killer final pass or shot, and so the score was still 0–0. What they needed was a moment of magic – a moment of Bruno magic. In the thirtieth minute, he won a free kick in a perfect position for one of his long-range rockets. But as he placed the ball down, Bruno had a better idea. He gave a quick signal to Anthony, who made a sprint towards goal, and Bruno delivered a delightful chip over the City defenders for him to hit on the volley. *1–0!*

Hurray, his clever plan had worked! The other United players raced over to congratulate their goalscoring duo as Old Trafford went wild all around them, singing the chant they had made up for their sensational new hero:

Bruno Bruno Bruno,
he's from Sporting like Cristiano.
He goes left, he goes right,

gives defences such a fright,
he's our Portuguese Magnifico!

'Thanks, you're a genius!' Anthony cheered, giving Bruno a big hug.

Talk about an instant impact! With two goals and three assists in his first five games, Bruno was already starring for his team and taking the Premier League by storm. The former United captain Roy Keane wasn't an easy man to impress but even he was full of praise: 'He has lifted everybody at the club. It is as if he has been there for twenty years. He has got pure quality and it looks like he is going to be a big player for United for the next few years.'

A few days later, Bruno received the Premier League Player of the Month prize for February to go with his Man of the Match award from the Manchester derby. But despite the big smiles, he was hungry for more. 'I'm happy with my start, but from now I need to give more to be better,' he said humbly.

What Bruno really wanted to win was the top team trophies – the Premier League title and the

Champions League. That's why he had moved to Manchester United in the first place.

CHAPTER 23

THE TIRELESS QUEST FOR TOP TROPHIES

'Come onnnnnnnnn!' Bruno cried out, sliding towards the corner flag on his knees.

With a skip and a jump, he had just scored another important penalty to give Manchester United the lead away at Leicester City on the final day of the 2019–20 season. Bruno was up to eight goals and seven assists in his first fourteen Premier League games – what a remarkable record! And more importantly, his team were now just twenty minutes away from finishing in the Top Four and qualifying for the Champions League again.

Bruno's brilliant start at Manchester United had come to a sudden stop in March, when the Premier

League season had to be suspended due to COVID-19. But after a long, three-month wait, he had got straight back to his brilliant best:

A penalty against Tottenham,

Two right-foot beauties against Brighton,

Two awesome assists against Bournemouth...

At that stage, United were still in fifth place in the Premier League table, but now, with one more win, they could leap above Leicester City and claim that crucial Champions League spot...

'Yesssssssssssssss!' Bruno yelled out as Jesse scored a last-minute second goal to secure the victory. Job done – 'Champions League, here we come!'

But before that, Bruno and his United teammates had the 2020 Europa League trophy to try and win. In extra-time in the quarter-final against FC Copenhagen, Anthony was fouled in the penalty area and up stepped Bruno to score the winner under pressure.

Goooooooooooooooooooaaaaaaaaaaaaaaaallllllllllllll llllllllllll!!!!!!!!!!!!!!!!!!

Six days later, Bruno scored another cool, calm spot-kick early in the semi-final against Sevilla, but sadly the Spanish club fought their way back into the game and with fifteen minutes to go, Luuk de Jong tapped in to give them a 2–1 lead.

'Hey, why weren't you marking him?' Bruno argued angrily with his teammate Victor Lindelöf. At the age of twenty-five, he was still the same bad loser he had always been. He was furious and frustrated with everyone: with the defenders for letting the goal in, with the attackers for wasting too many chances, and of course with himself too. He was supposed to be Manchester United's matchwinner and so he felt like he had failed.

At the final whistle, Bruno sat there on the pitch for a long time, staring down at the grass below his boots. How on earth had they lost that match? It didn't seem fair, and it certainly wasn't the way he wanted to end his fantastic first season at United. Winning the club's Player of the Year award was an amazing achievement, especially after only arriving in February, but a top team trophy was what he really wanted.

Oh well, at least Bruno had the Champions League to look forward to next season. He had played in the competition before, during his time at Sporting, but this would be different because United would be aiming to win it. Why not? Their team was full of world-class talent, from David de Gea in goal to their amazing array of attackers: Anthony, Marcus Rashford, Mason Greenwood, and new signing Edinson Cavani. Plus, in Bruno and Paul, they had two of the best playmakers in the game. So at their best, they knew that they were capable of beating anyone, even Neymar Jr and Kylian Mbappé's PSG.

But with Harry Maguire missing, United would need a new captain for their tricky away trip to Paris. David? Victor? Marcus? No, instead Solskjær handed the armband to his Portuguese midfield maestro, a player who was born to lead – Bruno!

Wow – when he heard the news, he couldn't believe it. He had only been at the club for six months! 'The first dream was playing for the club, and after that to play for the club as captain,' he said with a humble smile. 'It's such an honour.'

For Bruno, it really was a very proud moment, but he didn't feel any extra pressure. He was always a strong leader for his team anyway, whether he wore the armband or not.

'Let's go!' United's new captain called out to his teammates as they waited in the tunnel.

From the moment the match kicked off, Bruno was everywhere on the pitch: on the right, on the left, pushing forward, dropping deeper, wherever he needed to be to get the ball. And every time he got it, he looked to do something special with it:

A first-time flick to Marcus,

A quick one-two with Anthony,

A clever chest-down to Alex Telles,

A high, curling cross into the box.

A lot of the time, Bruno's creativity came to nothing, but that didn't bother him. He was competitive enough to track back and make up for his mistakes and courageous enough to keep on trying for the spectacular. Because it only took one moment of magic to make a difference. Midway through the first half, Anthony was fouled as he tried to spin away from his marker. *Another Manchester United penalty!*

Could Bruno step up and score from the spot yet

again? No! This time, the keeper guessed the right way and saved it. But wait – after checking with VAR, the referee ruled that the penalty had to be retaken because Keylor Navas had come off his line too early. Phew! Bruno was mightily relieved to get a second chance to score. Although the PSG players and supporters tried their best to put him off, the new United captain kept his cool. He even had the confidence to put his penalty in exactly the same place as last time! Only this time, Navas went the other way. *1–0!*

*Goooooooooooooooooooaaaaaaaaaaaaaaaaalllllllllllllll
lllllllllll!!!!!!!!!!!!!!!!!!!!*

'Yesssssssss!' Bruno shouted passionately, pumping his fists at the United fans.

Now, could his team hold on for a famous victory? Bruno chased all the way back to intercept a pass to Mbappé and then pushed United forward on the attack again. Tackles, blocks, passes, and shots – he was leading by example and the other players followed.

Even when PSG equalised early in the second half,

Bruno still believed that United could go on and win. 'Keep going!' he urged his teammates up the field, until eventually they got the goal they deserved. In the eighty-seventh minute, Paul played a pass to Marcus, who turned quickly into space and fired a shot into the bottom corner. *2–1!*

'YESSSSSSSSSS!' Ignoring his tired legs, Bruno raced over to join the team celebrations. It was a night that he would never forget – in his first match as captain, they had won away at PSG!

What a difference Bruno had made since joining Manchester United. His goals and assists changed games, his flicks and tricks entertained the crowd, but what really made the Portuguese playmaker so special was his winning mindset – his courage, confidence, leadership, and never-say-lose attitude. No wonder Bruno's United teammates now believed that they could win top trophies together. The Premier League, the Champions League, the Europa League; the FA Cup, the League Cup, the FIFA Club World Cup – with Bruno on the pitch, suddenly everything seemed possible.

Read on for a sneak preview of
another brilliant football story by
Matt and Tom Oldfield. . .

LEWANDOWSKI

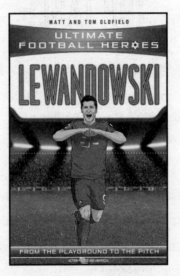

Available now!

CHAPTER 1

JOINING FOOTBALL'S TOP TABLE

17 December 2020

Robert paced from one side of the room to the other and could feel sweat trickling down the side of his cheek. Taking a deep breath, he wiped his cheek with the back of his hand. 'There's no reason to be nervous,' he told himself.

But, as much as he was a cool and calm finisher on the pitch, Robert always felt butterflies in his stomach on award nights. Plus, this was no ordinary awards night. Tonight, he was a finalist for FIFA Men's Player of the Year award, alongside Lionel Messi and Cristiano Ronaldo.

He caught a glimpse of himself in the hallway mirror and grinned. He had to admit – he looked good. His wife, Anna, had patiently helped him choose the perfect suit for this special occasion and it looked even better now than when he had first tried it on.

Just then, Robert's phone pinged twice. He walked over and scooped it up off the table. Due to health concerns, FIFA had decided to cancel the in-person awards show this year in favour of a video event – and these latest texts were from his FIFA representative, confirming that it would be another thirty minutes before he was added to the video call.

Robert sat down on the sofa and called Anna. 'Is it almost showtime?' she asked.

'Not quite,' he replied, laughing. 'But they've given me some amazing snacks while I wait.'

'Well, you can use the time to practise your speech. They say singing is a good way to warm up your voice!'

'No chance!' Robert replied, grinning. But he was feeling better now. Anna always knew how to calm him down.

As he caught up on her news and the latest updates from their daughters, the thirty minutes flew by. His phone buzzed with a new call from his FIFA representative, who had one quick message. 'Stand by – the TV crew want you on screen in two minutes.'

Robert had walked through the plan countless times with the FIFA team, yet he still felt a little shaky as he sat down in front of the camera, checked his microphone, and adjusted his earpiece. Thirty seconds and counting.

'It's time for the final award of the night,' the presenter explained. 'Over to you, Gianni.'

FIFA President Gianni Infantino appeared on the screen, walking down a hallway and clutching the trophy. He would be hand-delivering it to one of the three finalists for FIFA Men's Player of the Year – Messi, Ronaldo and Lewandowski. All three players were now on camera in the top part of the screen.

'And the winner is…' Gianni paused to build up the tension, then entered the room where Robert was sitting. '…Robert Lewandowski!'

Robert smiled as Gianni passed him the trophy. It

was heavier than he expected and looked a bit like the World Cup trophy. 'Thank you,' he said. 'This is a real honour.'

Then he turned to face the camera, just like he had been told during the rehearsal. 'I am very proud to have won this award. It was a team performance really and it was really impressive what we were able to win together. It's an incredible feeling and a privilege to be a finalist with Leo and Cristiano.'

Robert smiled as the voice in his earpiece told him he had another twenty seconds to wrap up his speech. 'This is a night that I will never forget. Thank you.'

As the presenters delivered their final words of the night, Robert's phone buzzed. 'That's a wrap. You're free to go.'

He let out a big breath and started to take off his bow tie. The messages from friends and family were now pouring in, congratulating him on his award. Anna sent a string of emojis – two hearts, a thumbs up and a trophy – from their daughter, Klara. 'She says "tell Daddy he was great",' Anna wrote.

Then came what felt like the hundredth FIFA text

of the night. 'One last thing – can you sign back into the event for a few more minutes?'

Even though he was eager to get home to his family, Robert did as he was told. The screen popped open again and he had to blink twice to believe his eyes. His childhood idol, Thierry Henry, was staring back at him. 'Whoaaaaa!'

'Congratulations!' Thierry said, laughing at Robert's shocked face. 'You deserve it. You were outstanding and you've been outstanding for a long time. It takes something special to finish ahead of Leo and Cristiano – and you did it.'

Robert was speechless. 'Thank you,' he finally managed to reply. 'This means so much to me.'

What a night, and what a season. Robert had fired Bayern Munich to an unstoppable Champions League-Bundesliga-German Cup Treble, scoring a sensational fifty-five goals along the way, and this major individual honour was the icing on the cake. This year, he had risen to the top table of world football, and tonight he had confirmed it.

As he chatted to Thierry, Robert saw his whole

career flash before his eyes. The boy who was once called 'too skinny' and 'too weak' now had more trophies than he could have ever dreamed of. There had been plenty of difficult moments along the way when Robert could have simply walked away, but he refused to give up.

With the shiny trophy tucked under his arm, Robert knew he was now being rewarded for overcoming those obstacles. He reflected once again on how proud he was to have done it the hard way.

FERNANDES HONOURS

Sporting Lisbon
🏆 Portuguese League Cup: 2017–18, 2018–19
🏆 Portuguese Cup: 2018–19

Portugal
🏆 UEFA Nations League: 2018–19

Individual
🏆 Primeira Liga Player of the Year:
2017–18, 2018–19
🏆 UEFA Nations League Finals Team of the
Tournament: 2019

🏆 UEFA Europa League top scorer: 2019–20
🏆 Manchester United Player of the Year: 2019–20
🏆 Premier League Player of the Month:
February 2020, June 2020, November 2020,
December 2020

FERNANDES

18

THE FACTS

NAME:
Bruno Miguel Borges
Fernandes

DATE OF BIRTH:
8 September 1994

AGE: 26

PLACE OF BIRTH: Maia

NATIONALITY: Portugal

BEST FRIEND: Bernardo Silva

CURRENT CLUB: Manchester United

POSITION: CAM

THE STATS

Height (cm):	179
Club appearances:	364
Club goals:	122
Club trophies:	3
International appearances:	27
International goals:	2
International trophies:	1
Ballon d'Ors:	0

★ ★ ★ **HERO RATING: 88** ★ ★ ★

GREATEST MOMENTS

6 APRIL 2013,
NOVARA 3–2 SASSUOLO

At the age of only eighteen, Bruno broke into the Novara first team and helped lead the team from lower mid-table all the way to the Serie B play-off places. Early on in this crucial win over the league leaders Sassuolo, Bruno showed off his talent and strong character by firing a shot from thirty yards out into the top corner. Another moment of magic from the 'Maradona of Novara'!

★2 25 MAY 2019, SPORTING LISBON 2–2 PORTO (SPORTING WON ON PENALTIES)

Bruno capped off the best season of his career by leading Sporting to two trophies. A second League Cup win was lovely, but the Portuguese Cup was the one that he really wanted, especially after losing in the final the previous year. Bruno scored twice this time – once in the match and once in the penalty shoot-out – and he even got to lift the cup first as Sporting's superstar captain.

★3 9 JUNE 2019, PORTUGAL 1–0 NETHERLANDS

Bruno and Bernardo Silva were Portugal's stand-out stars in this UEFA Nations League final. With their clever passing and movement, the two playmakers linked up again and again, and Bruno was really unlucky not to score. Instead, it was Gonçalo Guedes who grabbed the winner to give Bruno his first international trophy.

4 20 OCTOBER 2020, PSG 1–2 MANCHESTER UNITED

It was Marcus Rashford who scored the winner in this huge Champions League match, but United couldn't have done it without their new captain – Bruno! He was everywhere for his team and he even opened the scoring from the penalty spot. His first attempt was saved, but Bruno got a second chance, which he calmly and confidently put in exactly the same place, only this time, the keeper dived the other way.

5 24 JANUARY 2021, MANCHESTER UNITED 3–2 LIVERPOOL

Solskjær decided to start Bruno on the subs bench for this FA Cup Fourth Round clash, which made him even more determined to come on and change the game. With the score tied at 2–2 and only fifteen minutes to go, he stepped up and scored a fantastic free kick. Once again, Bruno was Manchester United's matchwinner!

PLAY LIKE YOUR HEROES

THE BRUNO FERNANDES
LONG-RANGE ROCKET

STEP 1: Push your team forward on the attack with your clever passing and constant movement. Left wing, right wing, in the midfield – make it impossible for anyone to mark you.

STEP 2: What you're searching for is a pocket of space somewhere outside the penalty area – your danger zone. Once you find it, call quickly and loudly for the ball. Your teammates will listen; they know all about your long-range rockets.

STEP 3: While you wait for the pass, look up for one final scan of the space around you and the goal in front of you, so that as soon as it arrives, you're ready to act fast.

STEP 4: If you need to, take a touch to control the ball, or dribble a little closer to the target. But don't be scared to strike it straight away; the earlier you shoot the better, because you might catch the keeper by surprise.

STEP 5: BANG! Strike the ball with power, so that it either skids towards the bottom corner, or swerves and dips into the top corner. Whichever looks most likely to lead to a...

STEP 6: ...GOAL! Slide towards the corner flag on your knees with a big smile on your face, and let the fans adore you.

TEST YOUR KNOWLEDGE

QUESTIONS

1. Name at least two of Bruno's earliest football heroes.

2. As well as central midfield, what other position did Bruno often play when he was young?

3. Aged fourteen, Bruno refused to leave Portugal and move to which other European country with his family?

4. How old was Bruno when he made his brave move to Italy?

5. What nickname did the local newspapers give Bruno during his first season there?

6. Name at least two of Bruno's later midfield heroes.

7. Which shirt number did Bruno wear at Sporting?

8. At Sporting, Bruno formed a brilliant partnership with which tall Dutch target man?

9. Who scored Portugal's winning goal in the UEFA Nations League final in 2019?

10. Which shirt number did Bruno choose at Manchester United, once worn by Paul Scholes?

11. Which other English club did Bruno nearly sign for during the summer of 2019?

1. Any of the following: his brother Ricardo, his cousin Vítor, Ronaldinho and Cristiano Ronaldo. 2. Central defence. 3. Switzerland. 4. Seventeen. 5. The 'Maradona of Novara'. 6. Any of João Moutinho, Andrés Iniesta, Andrea Pirlo, and Paul Scholes. 7. Number 8. 8. Bas Dost. 9. Gonçalo Guedes. 10. Number 18. 11. Tottenham.